Mandala

Colouring Book

#1

Evelyn Whitebear

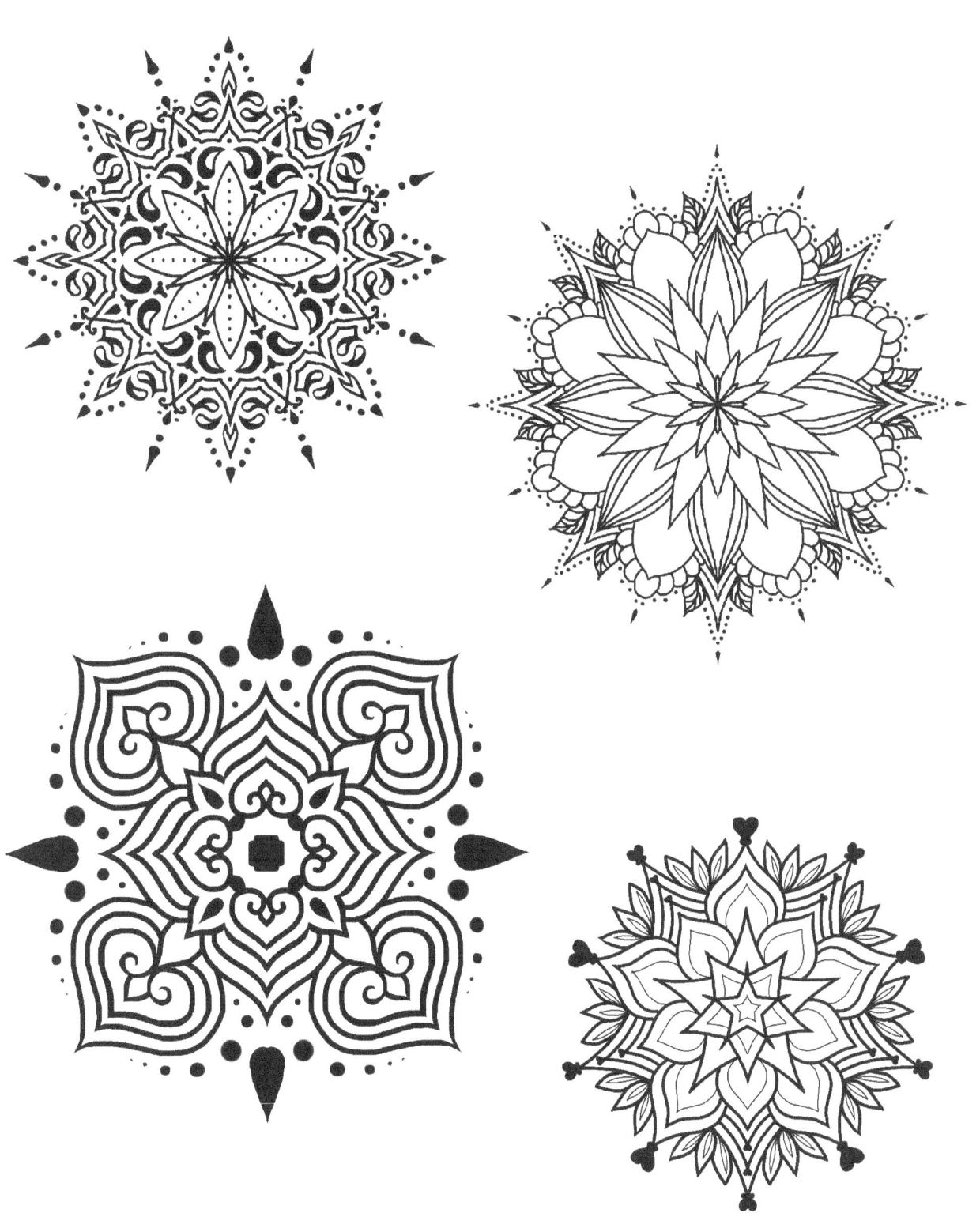

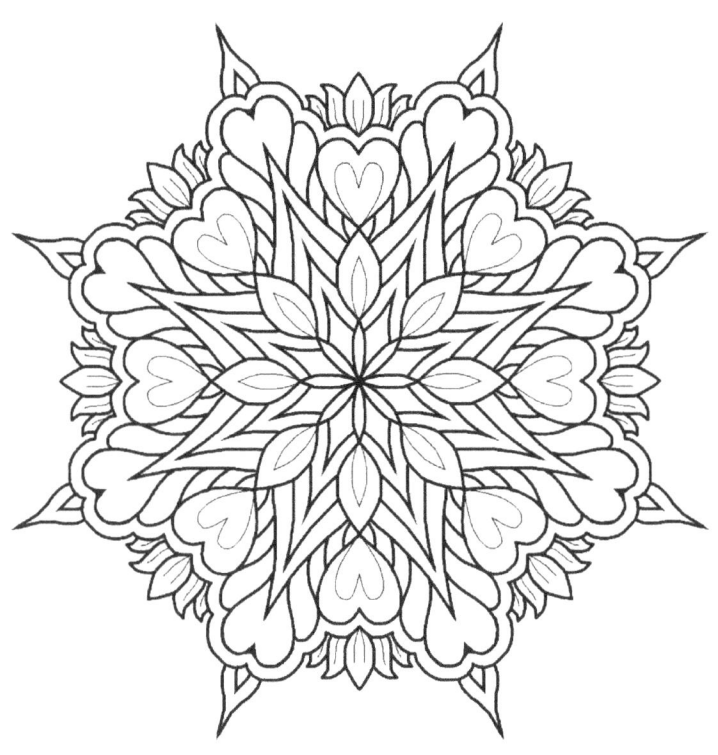

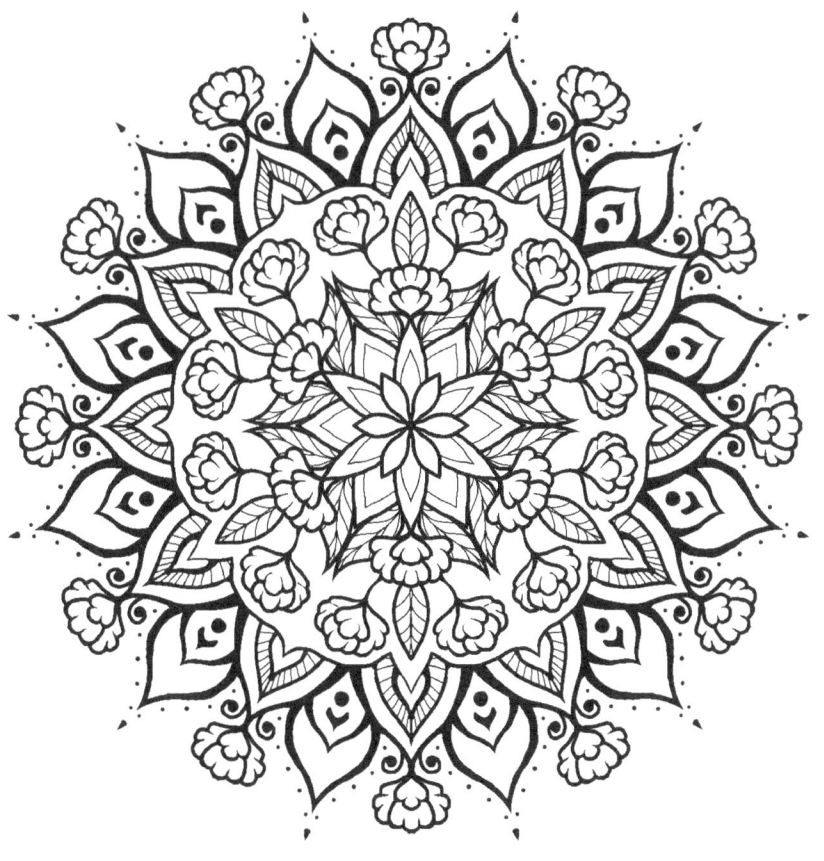

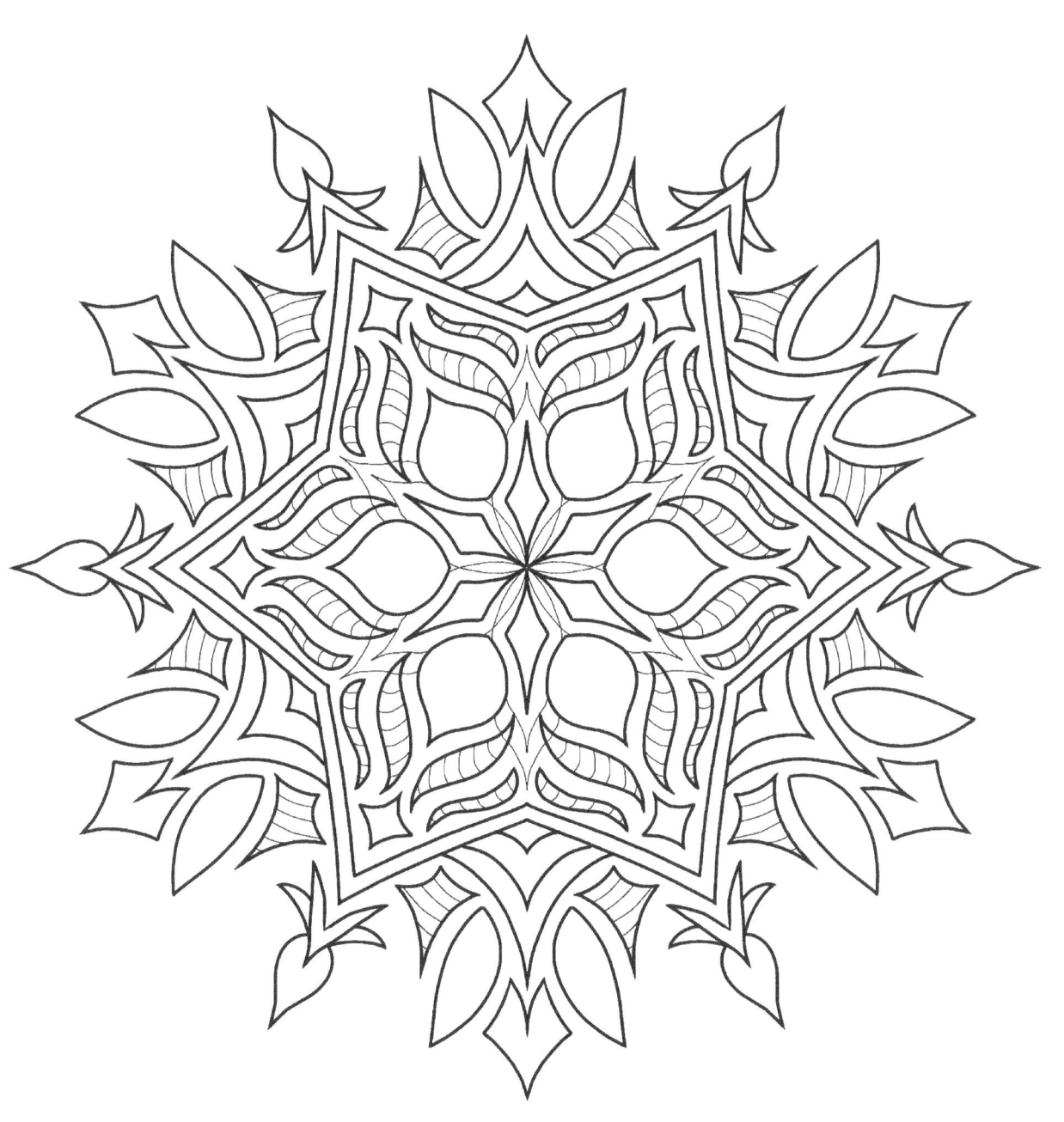

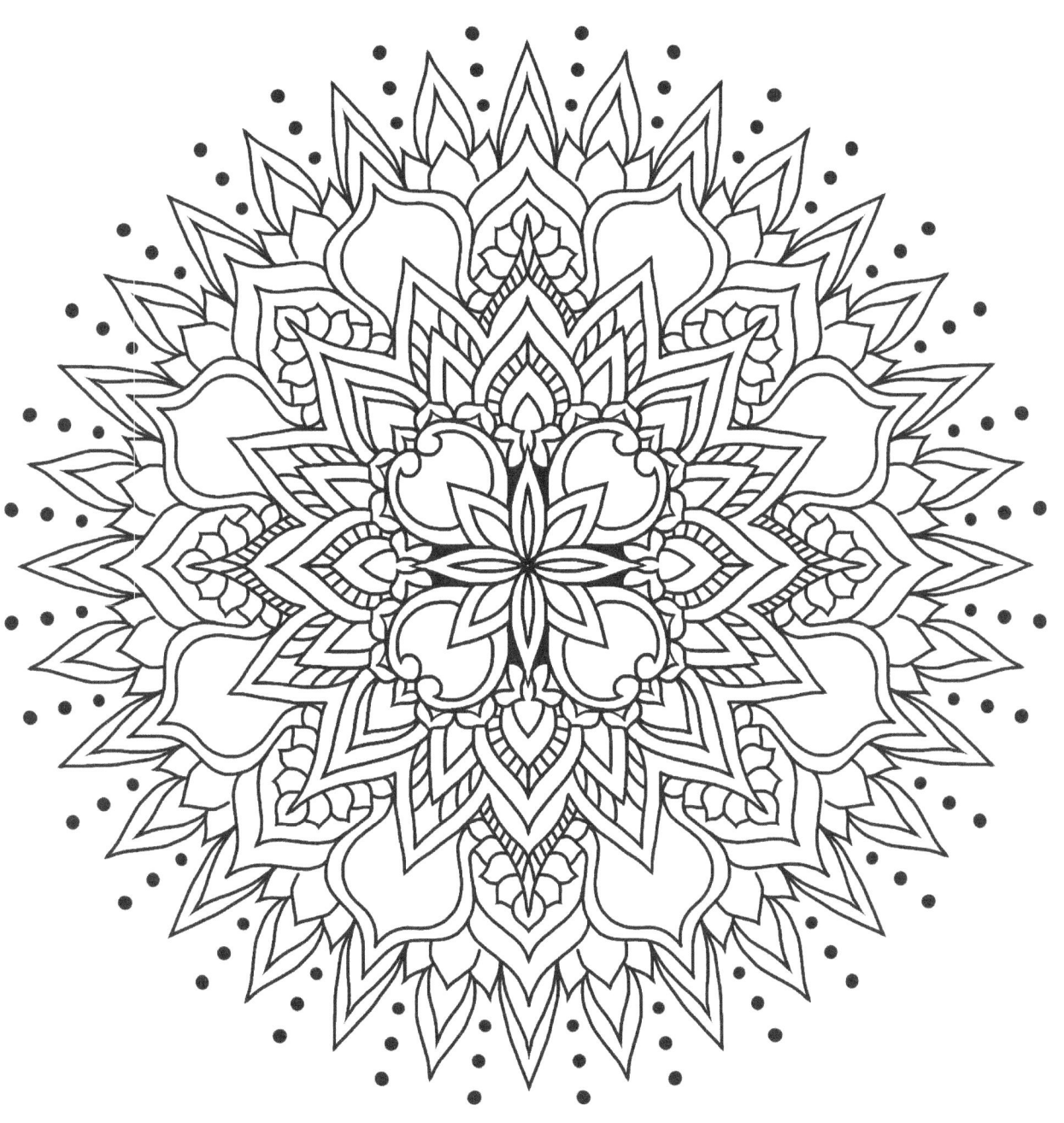

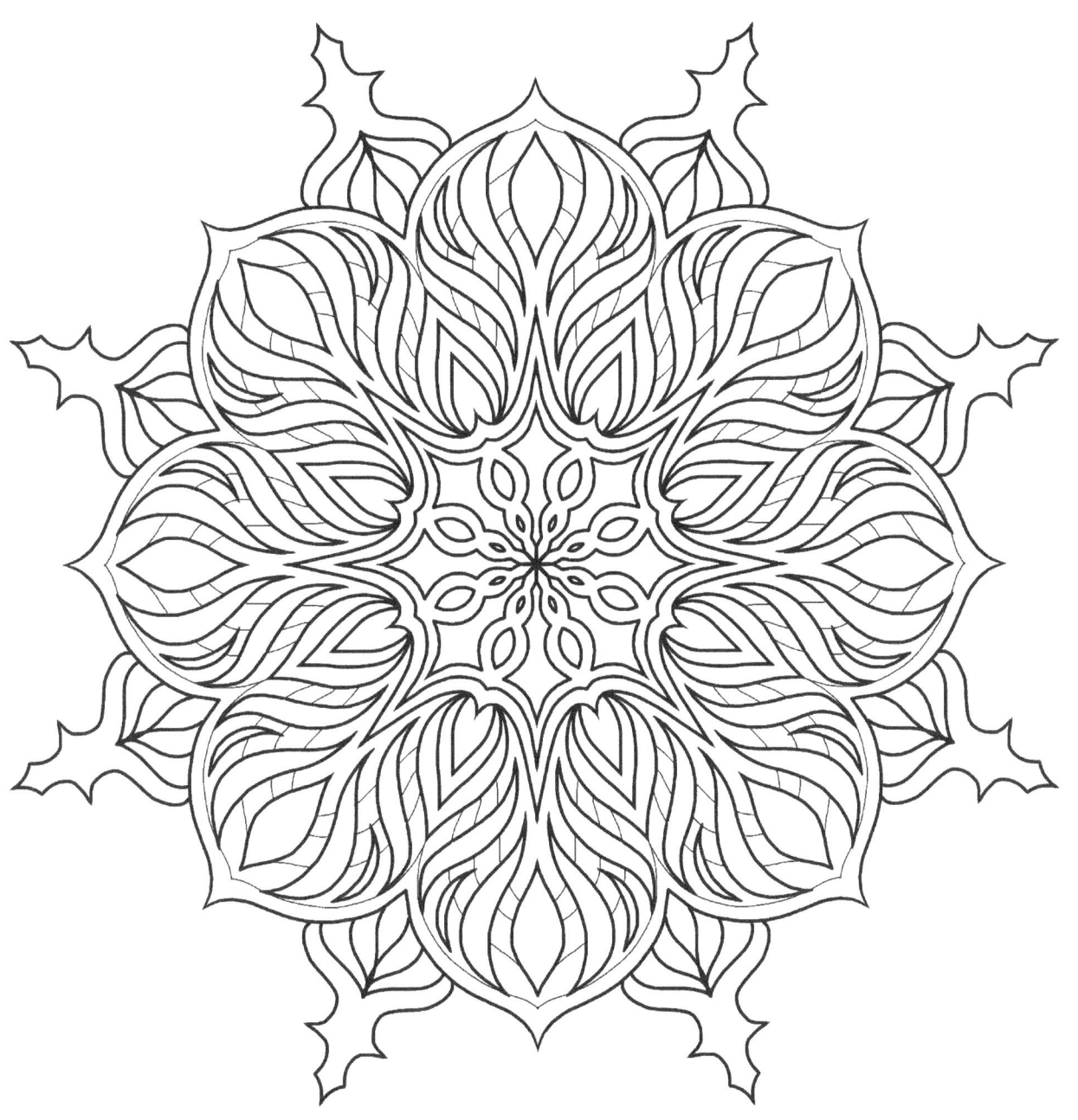

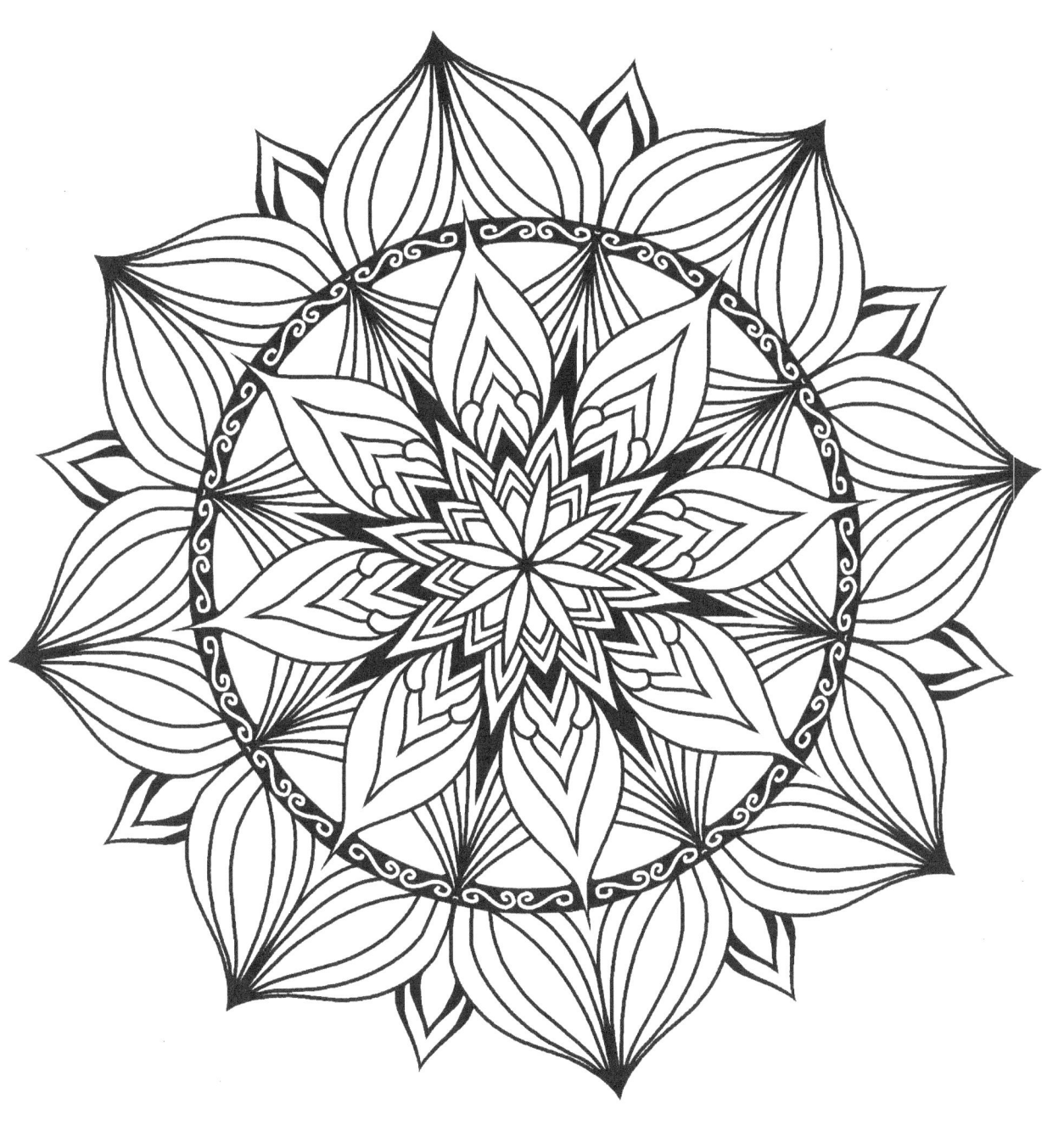

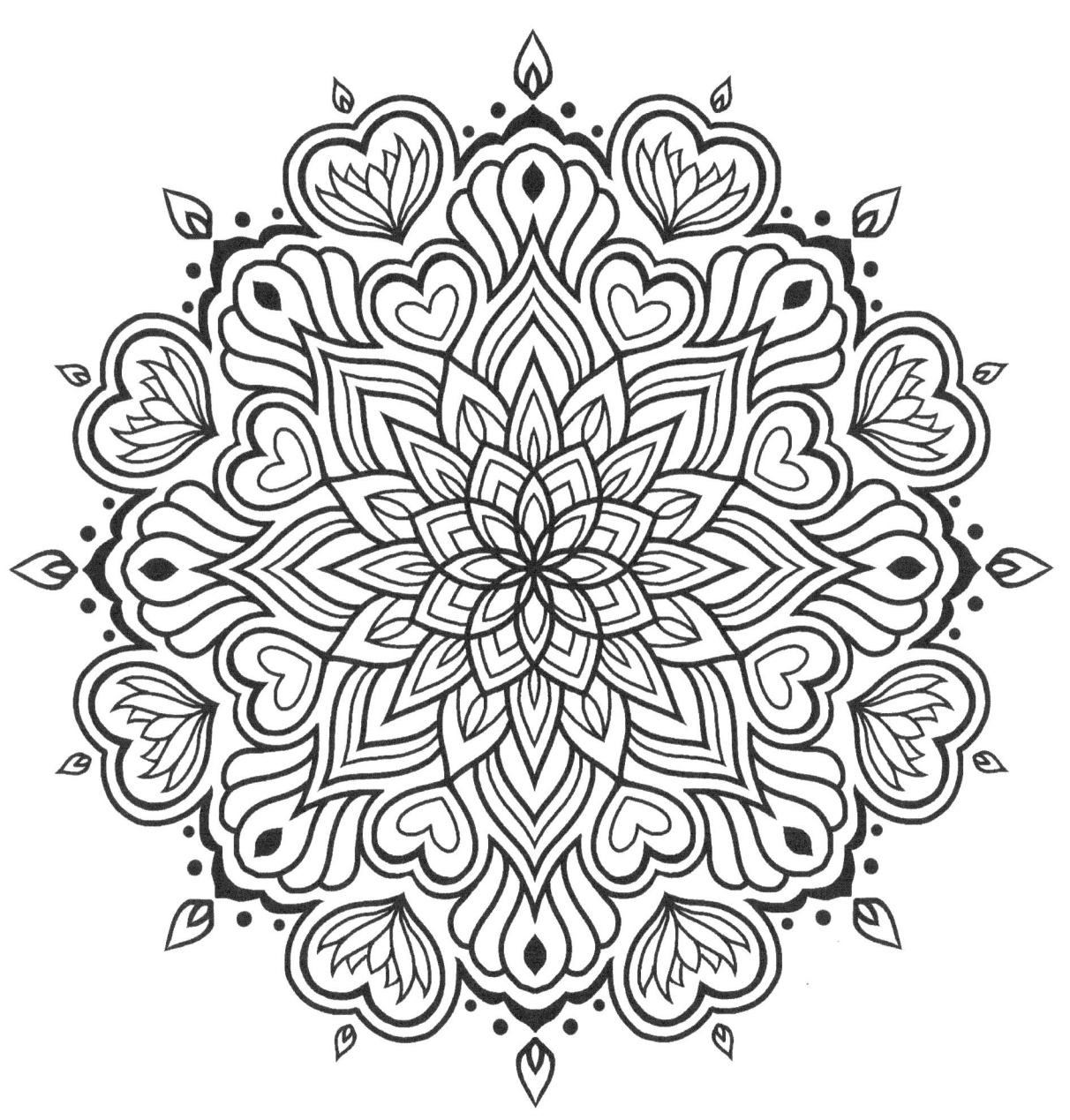

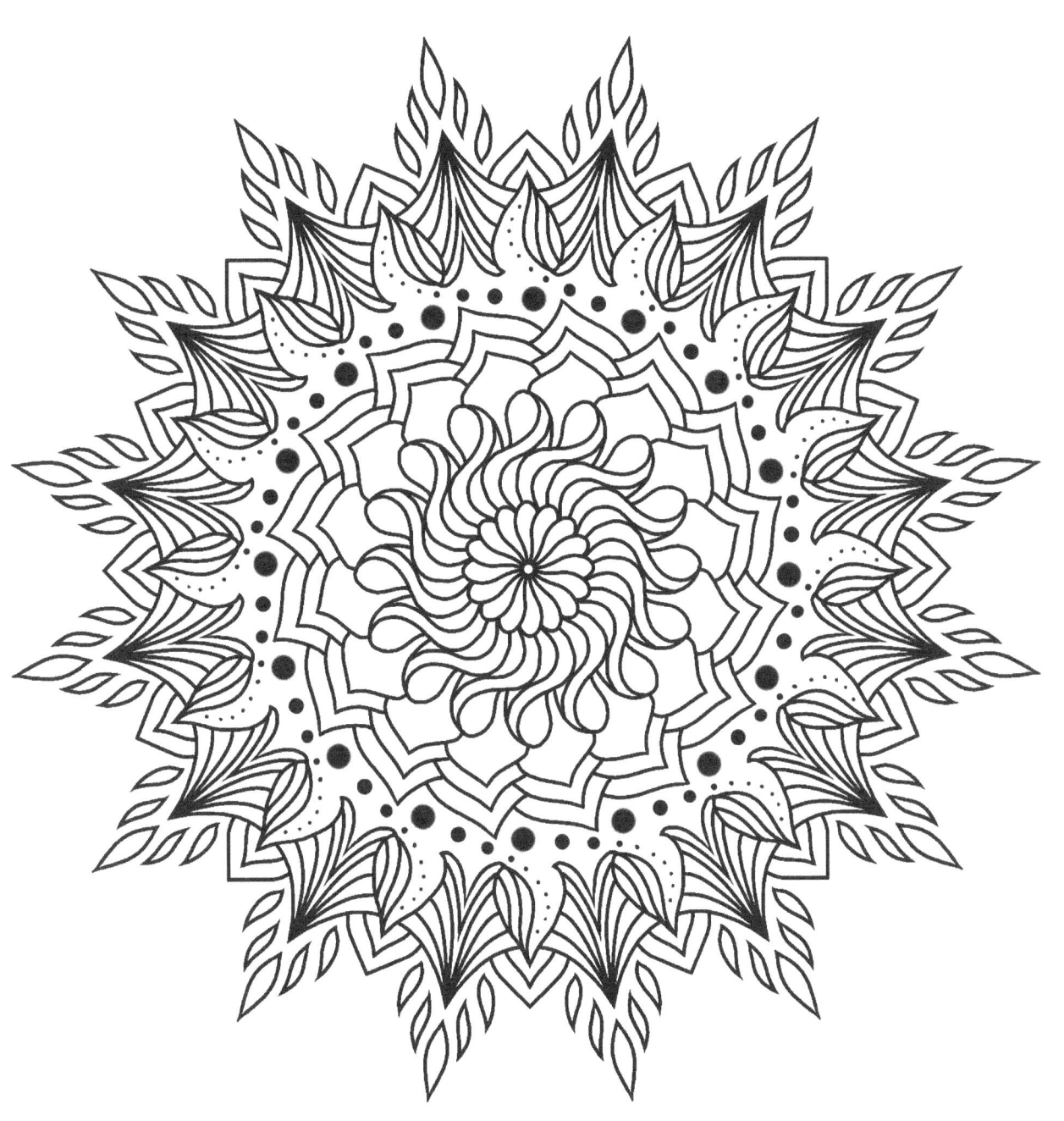

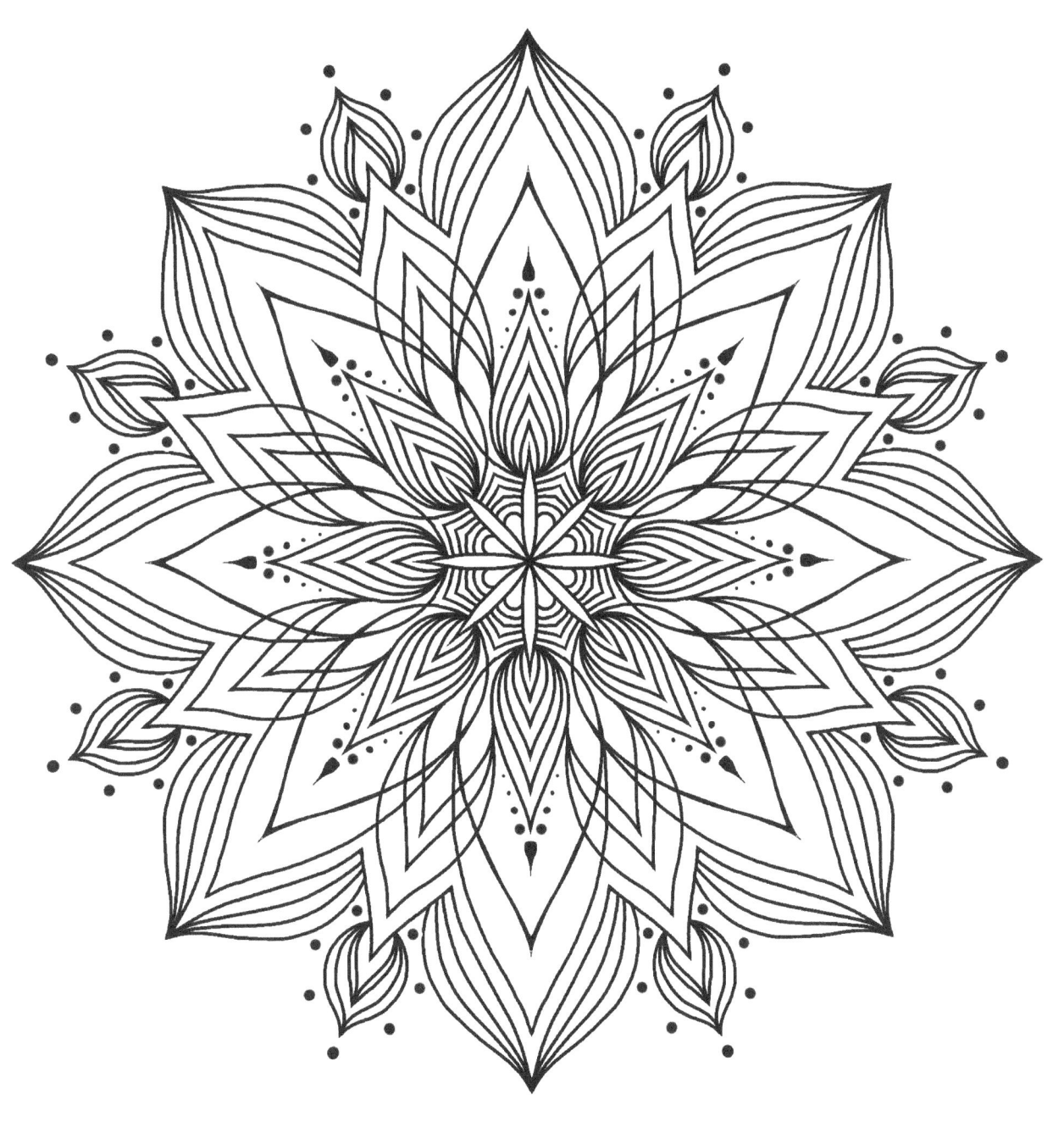

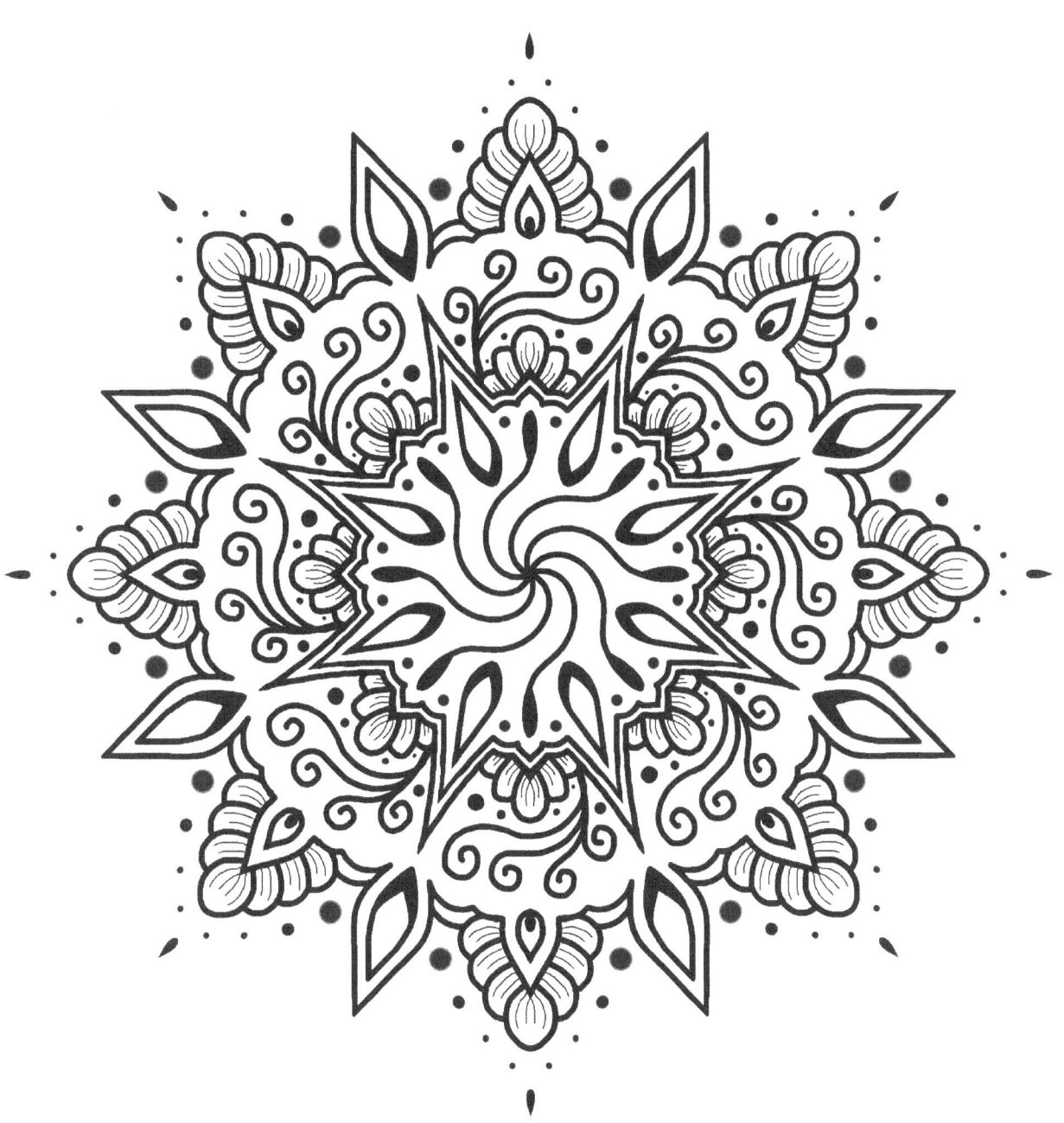

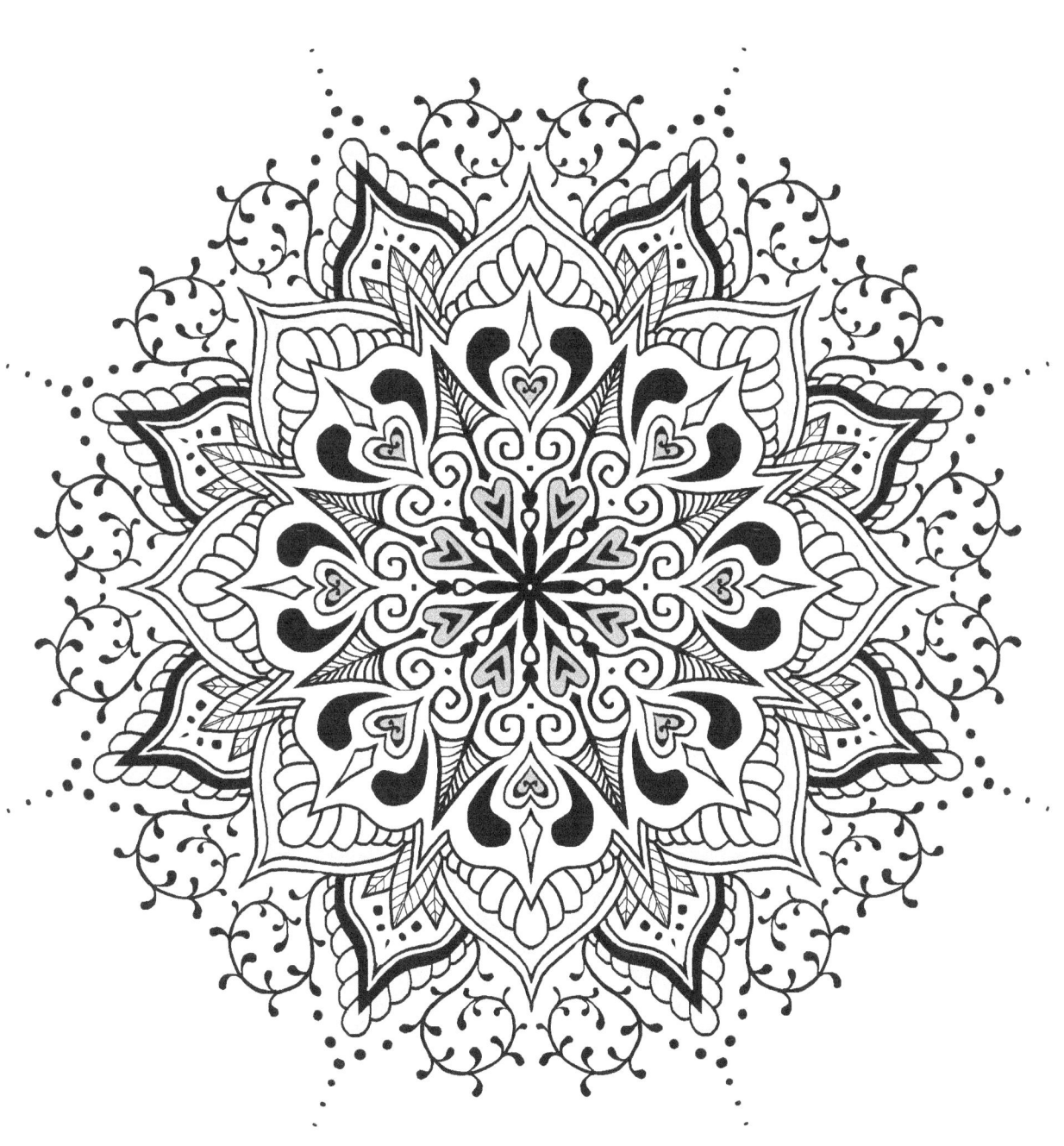

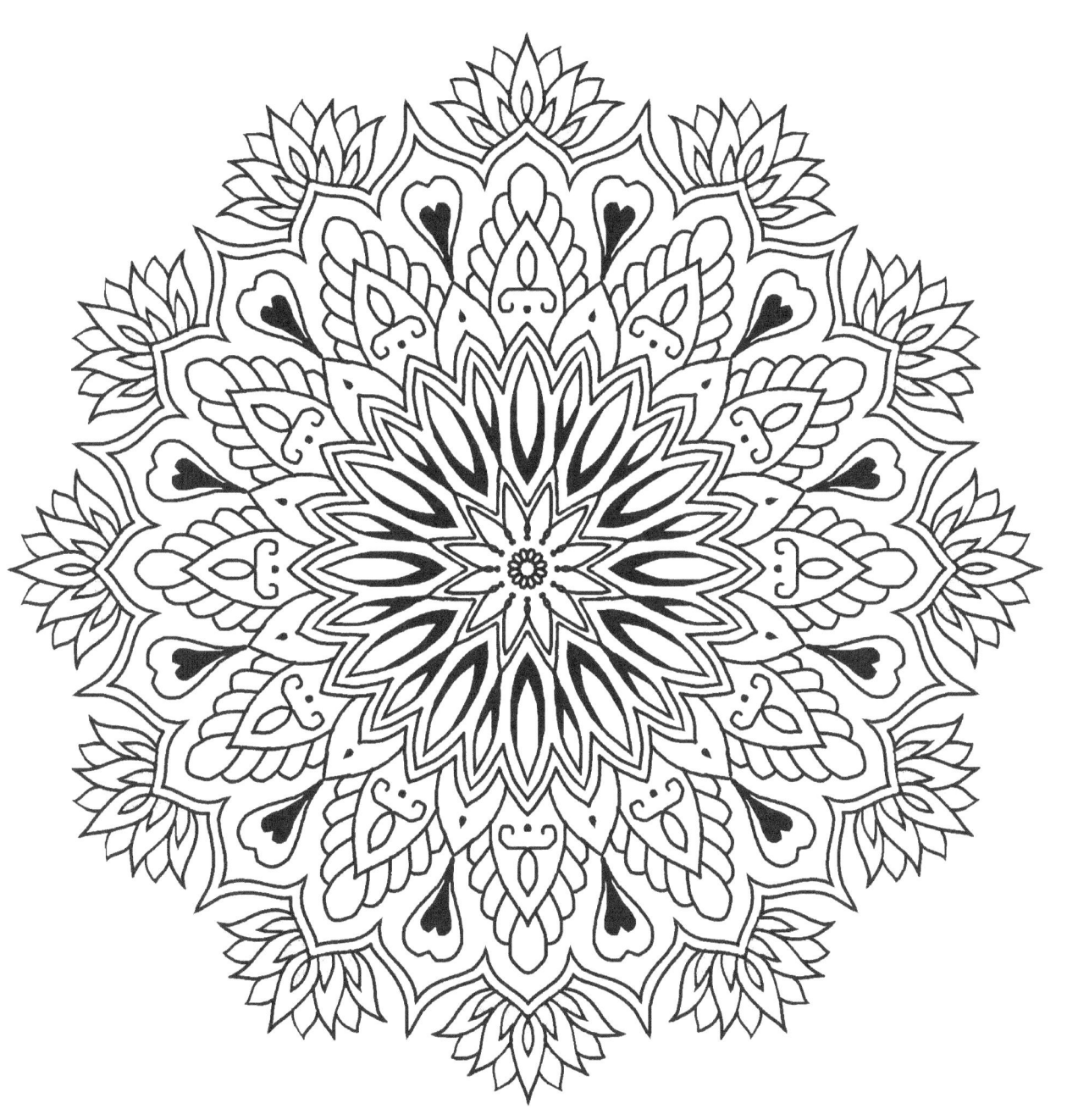

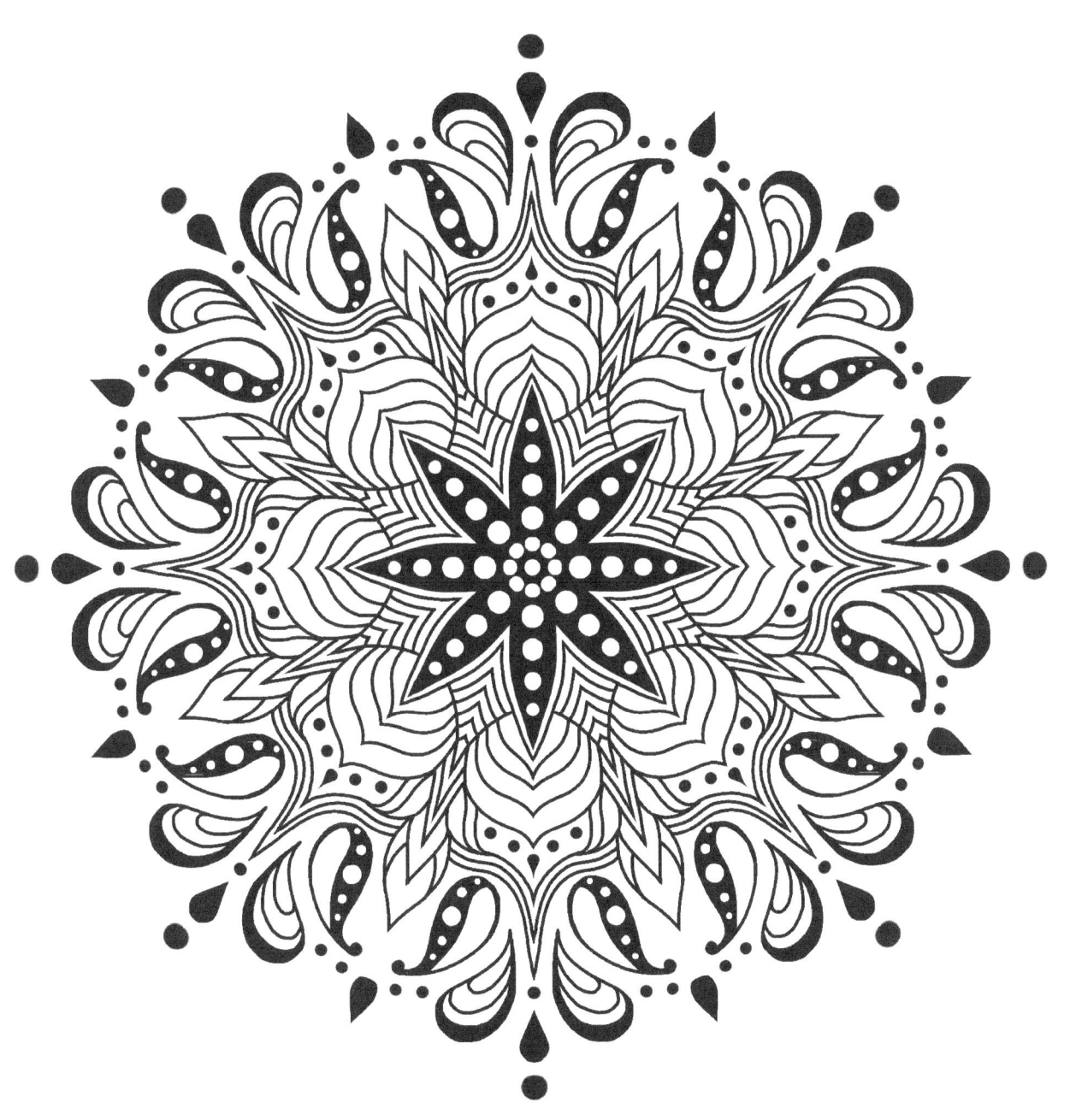

© Evelyn Whitebear, 2017

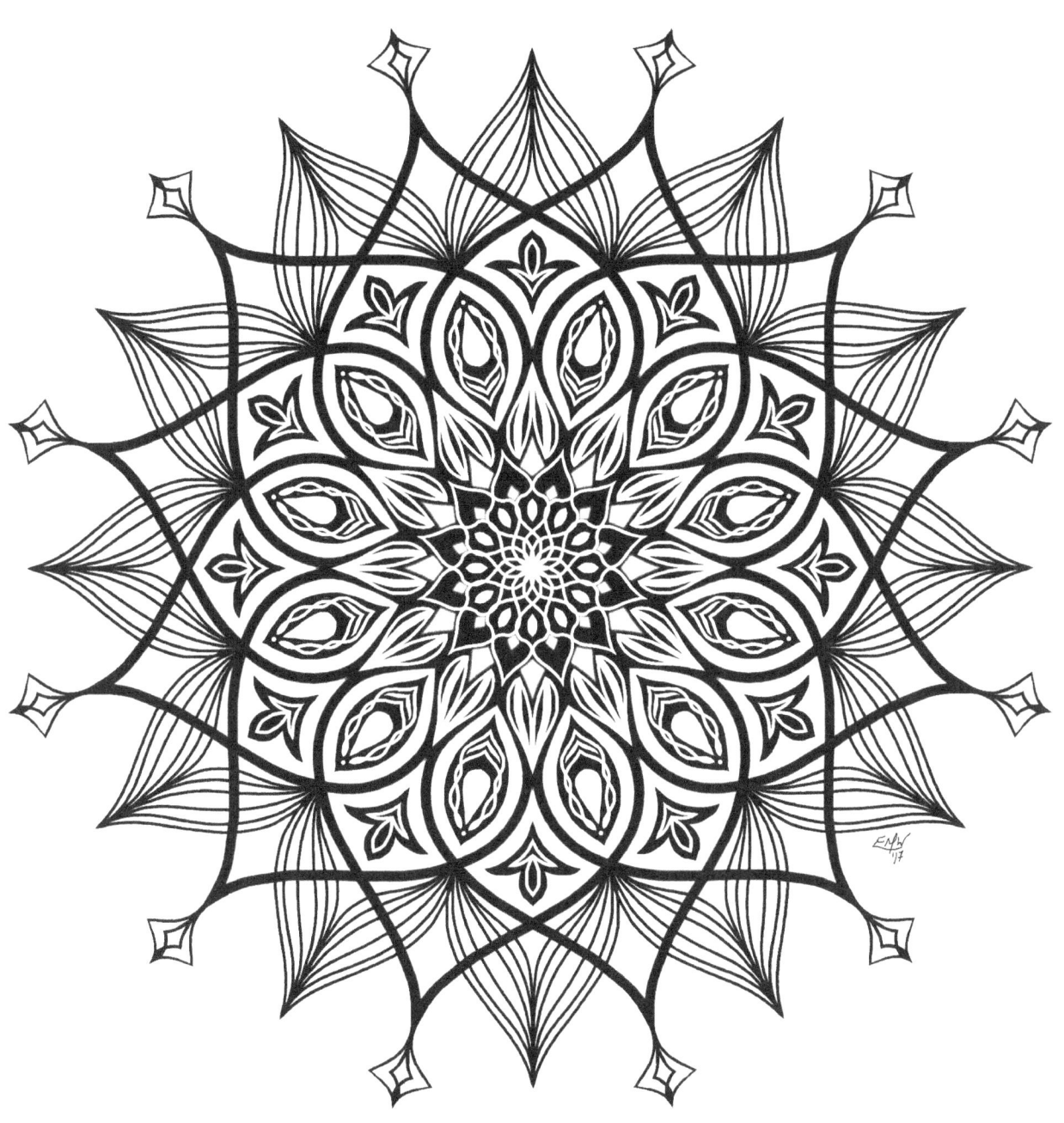

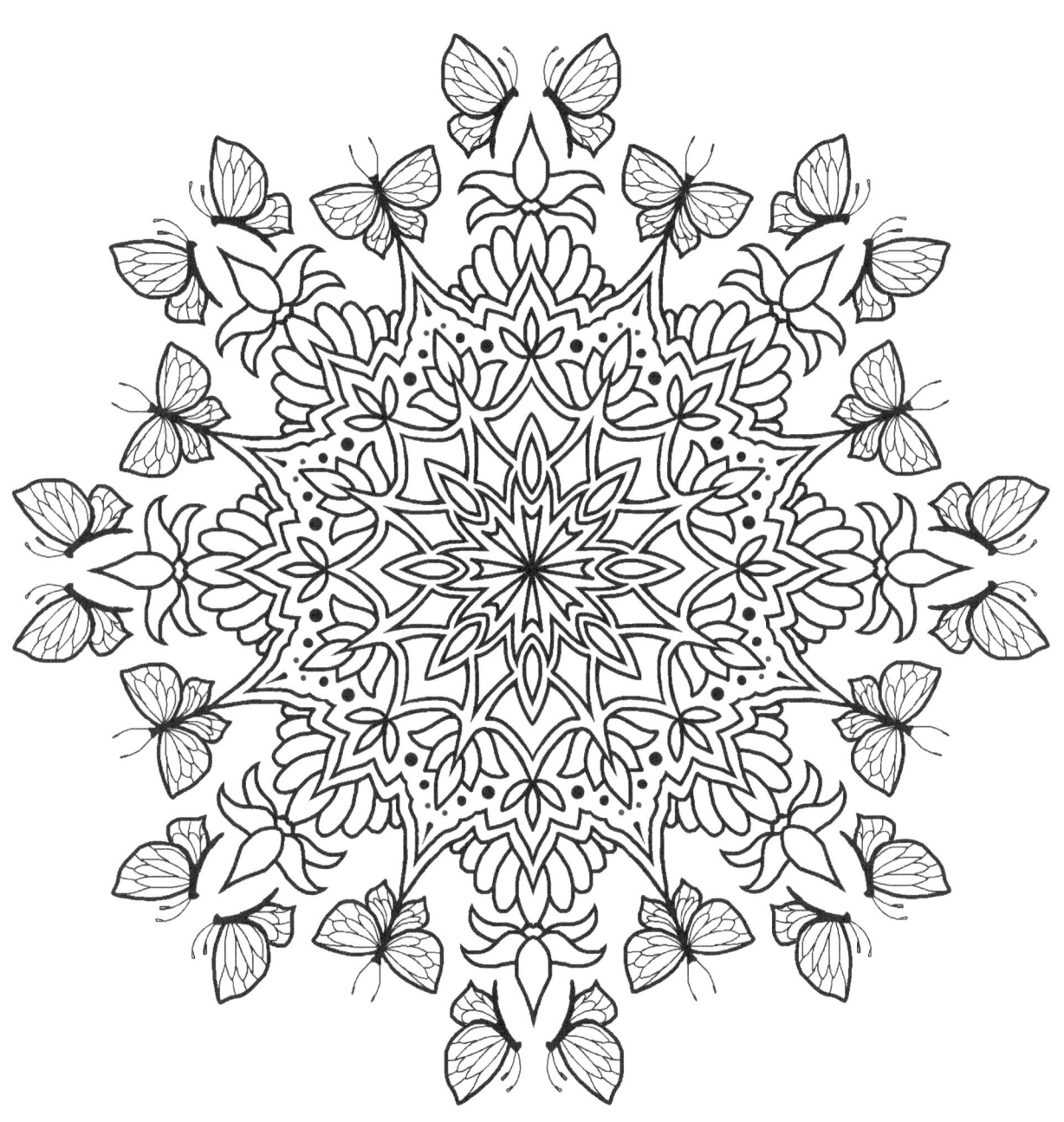

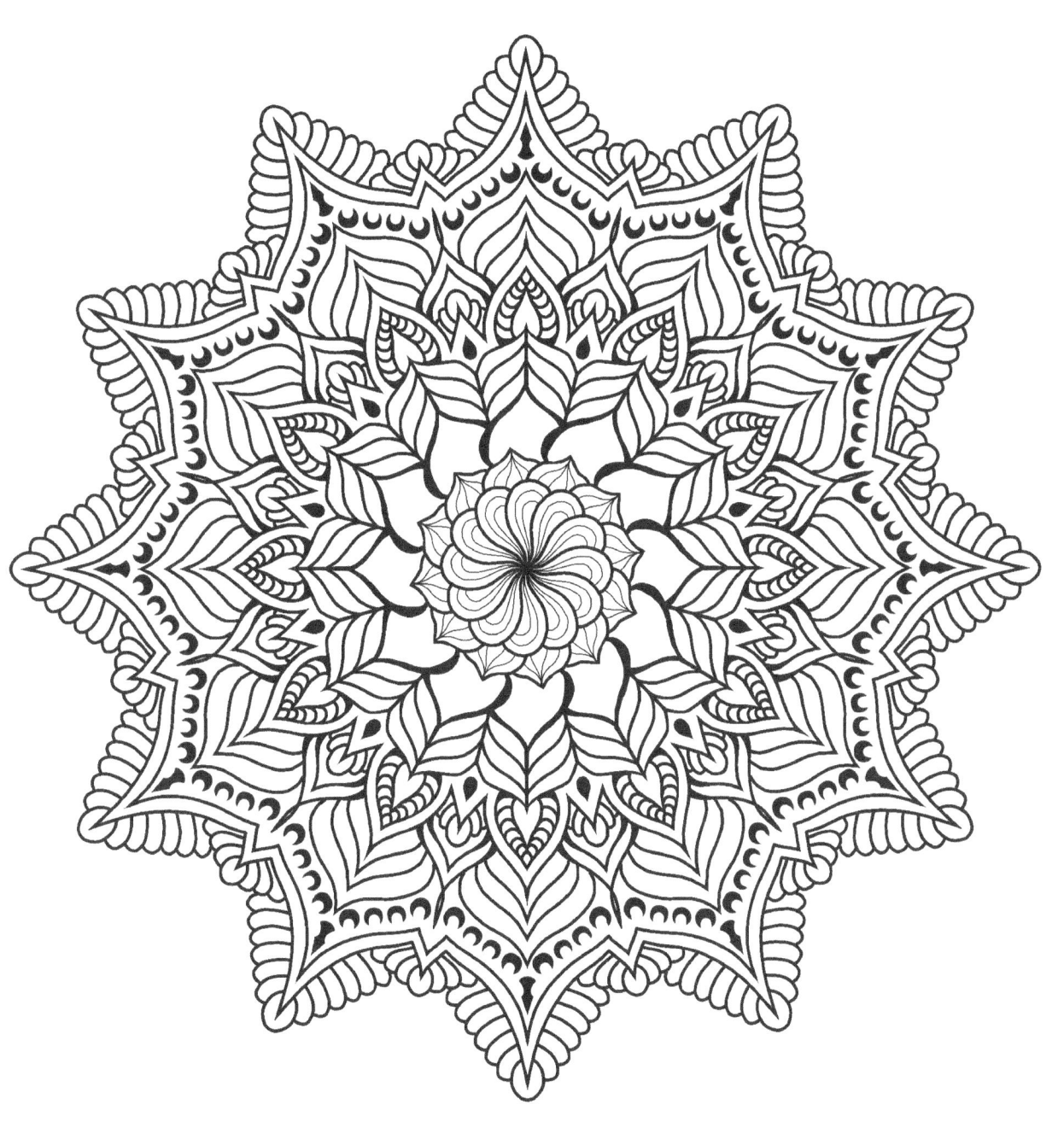

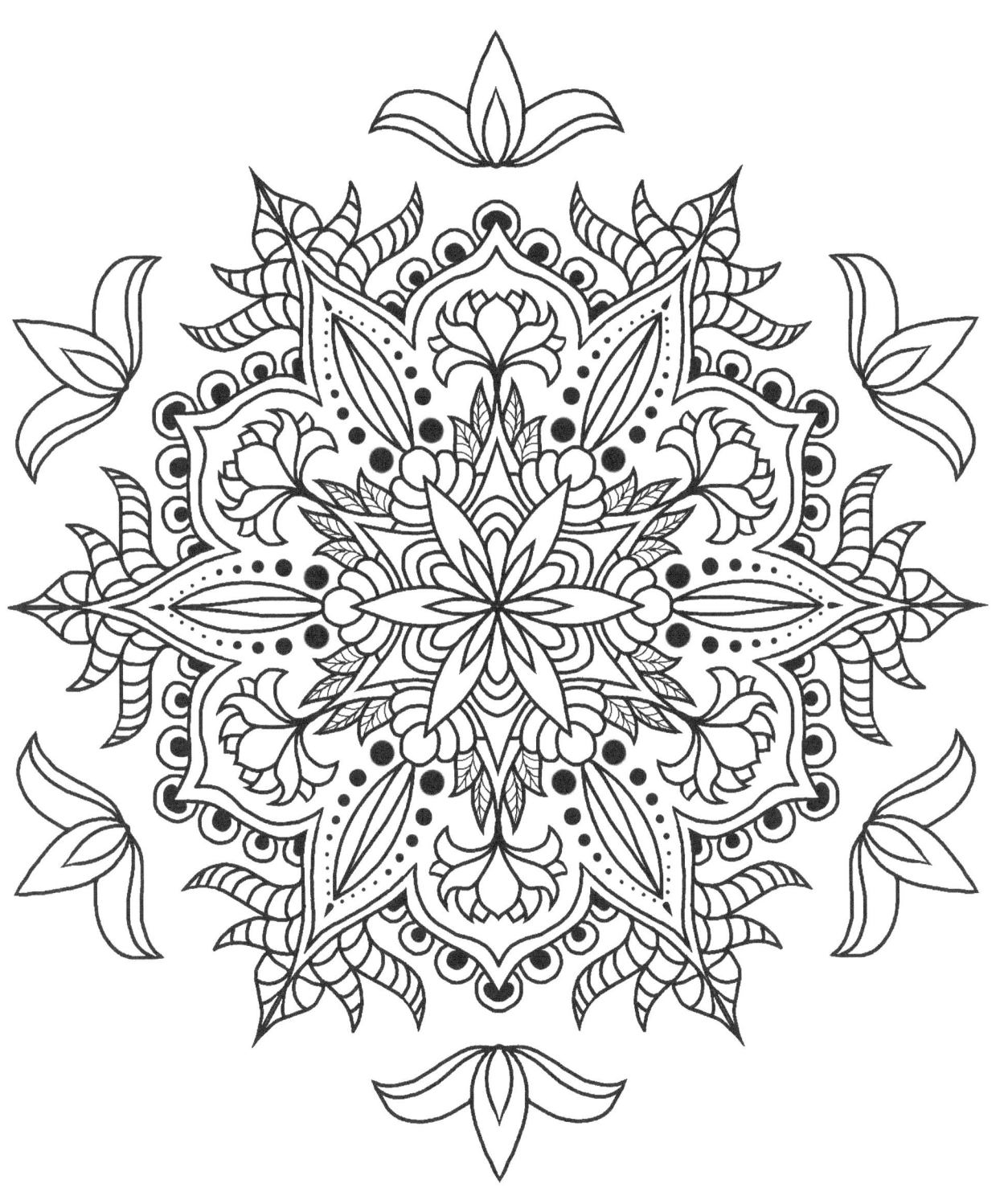

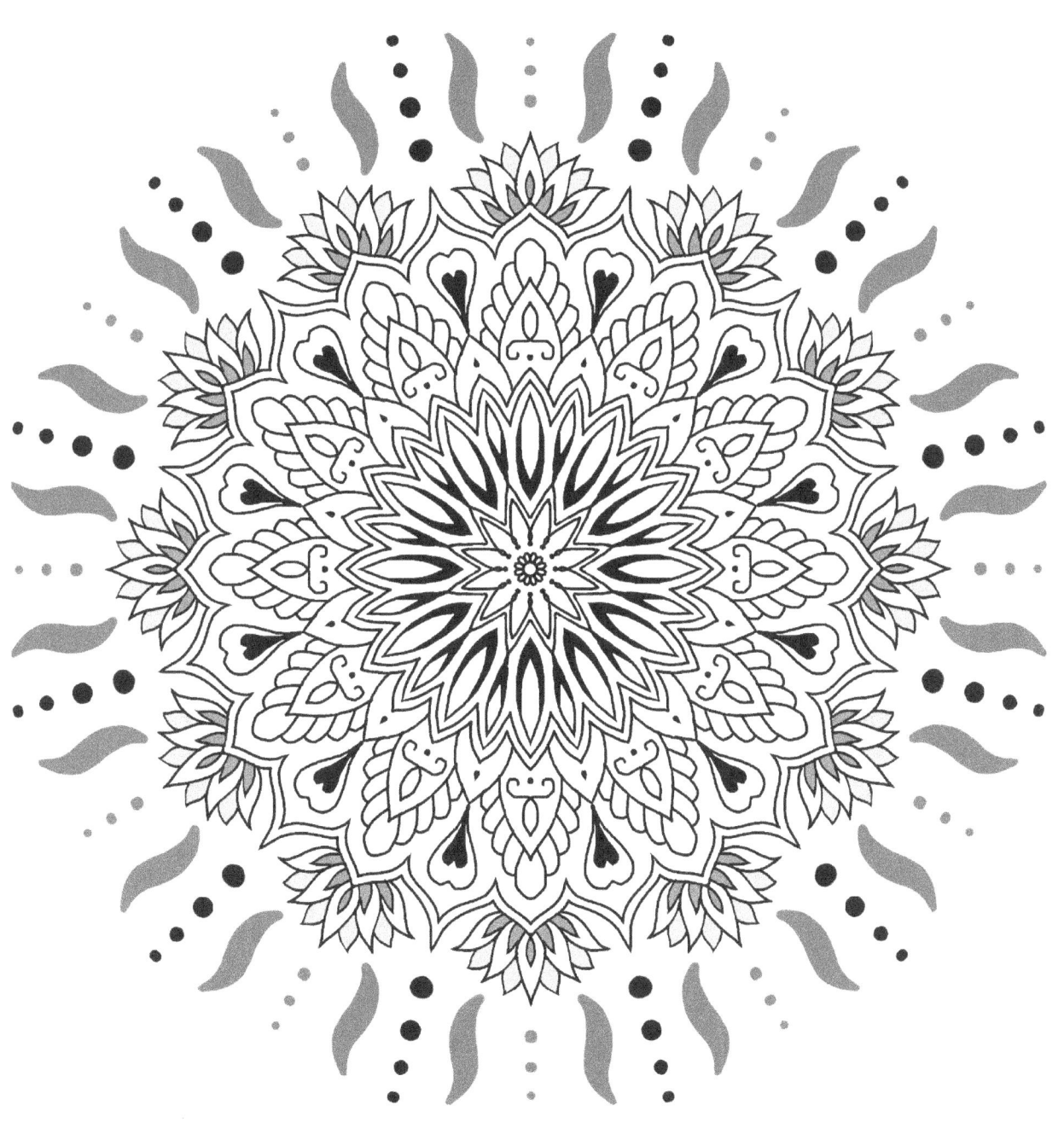

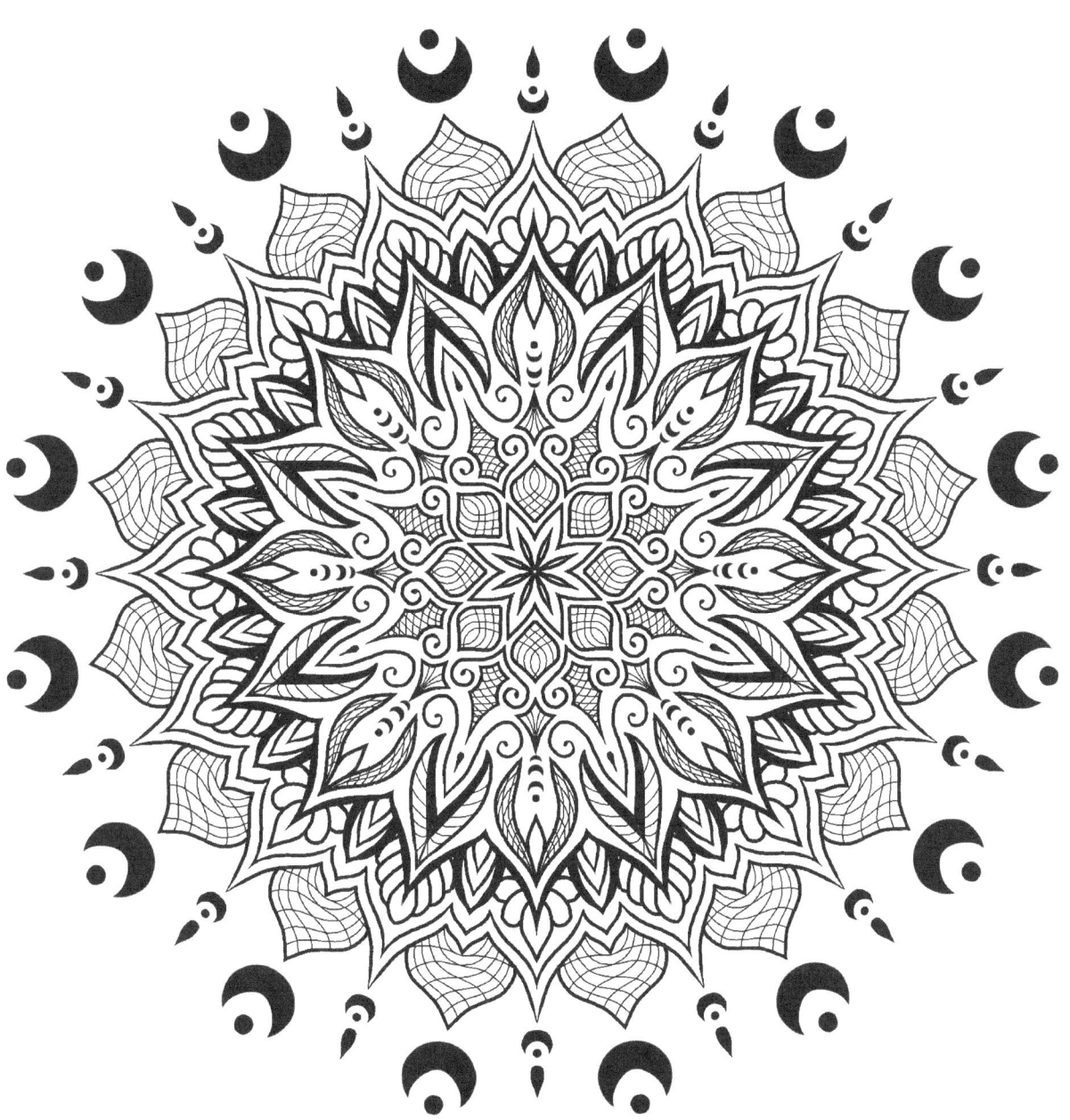

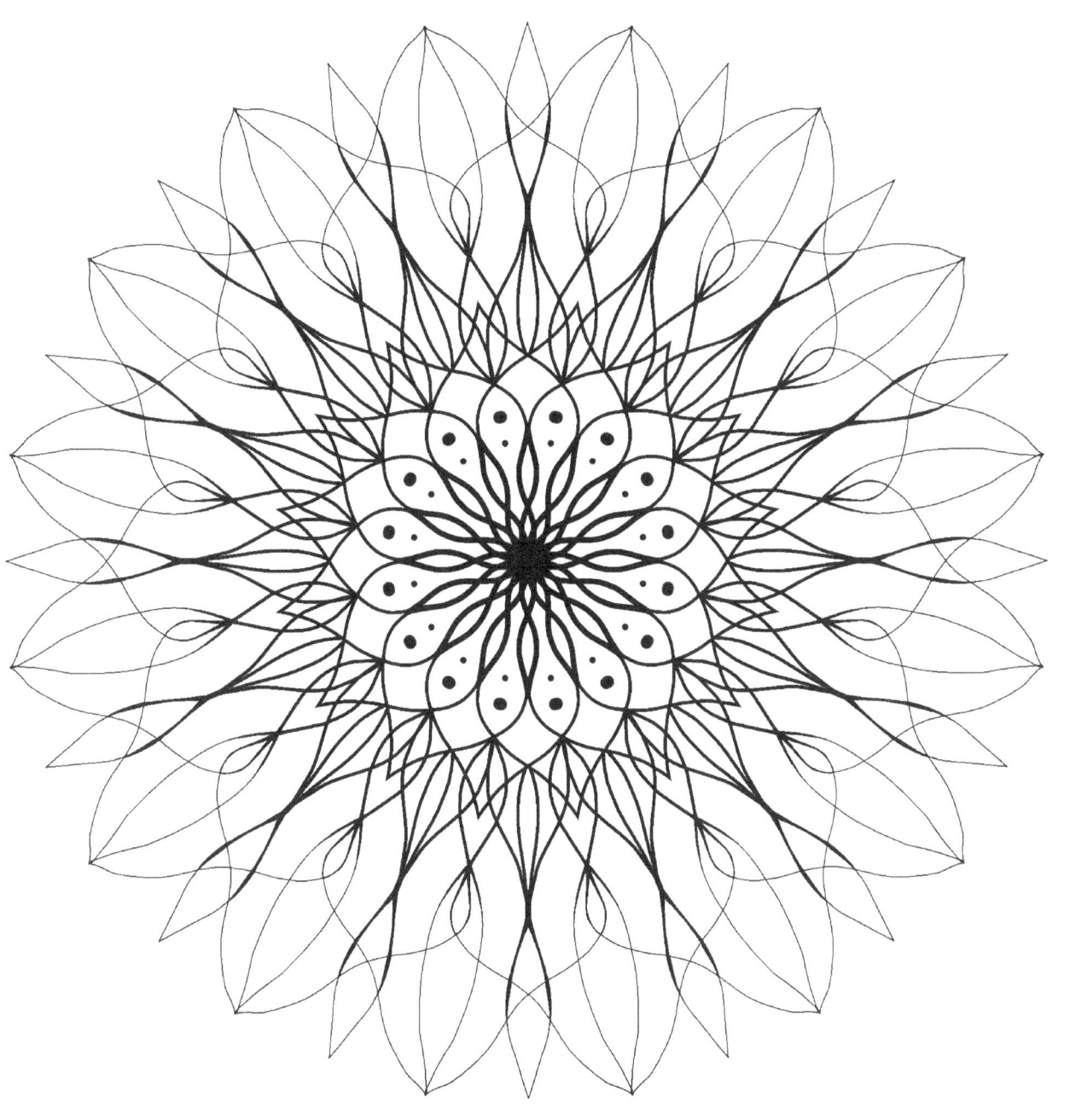

© Evelyn Whitebear, 2017

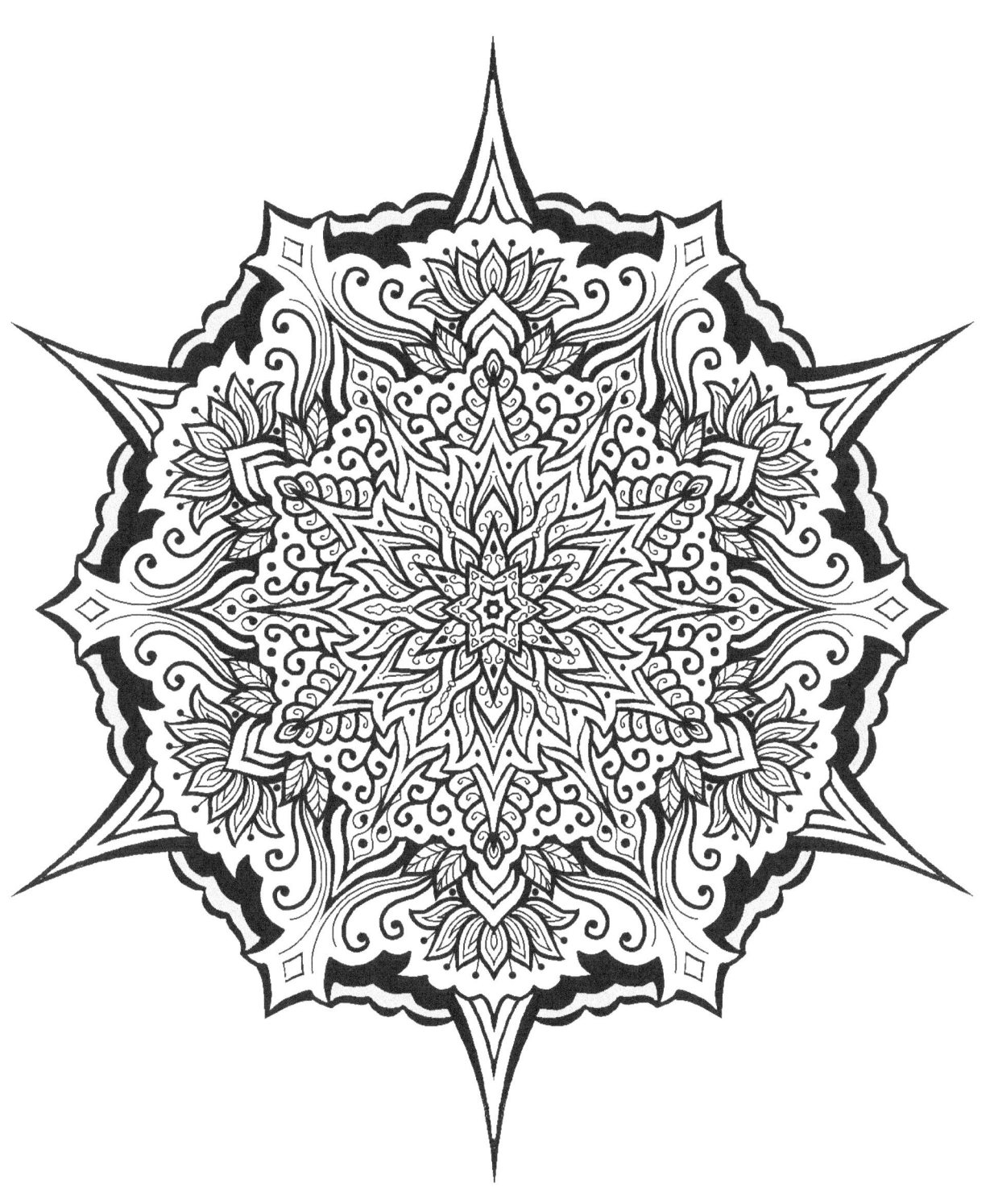

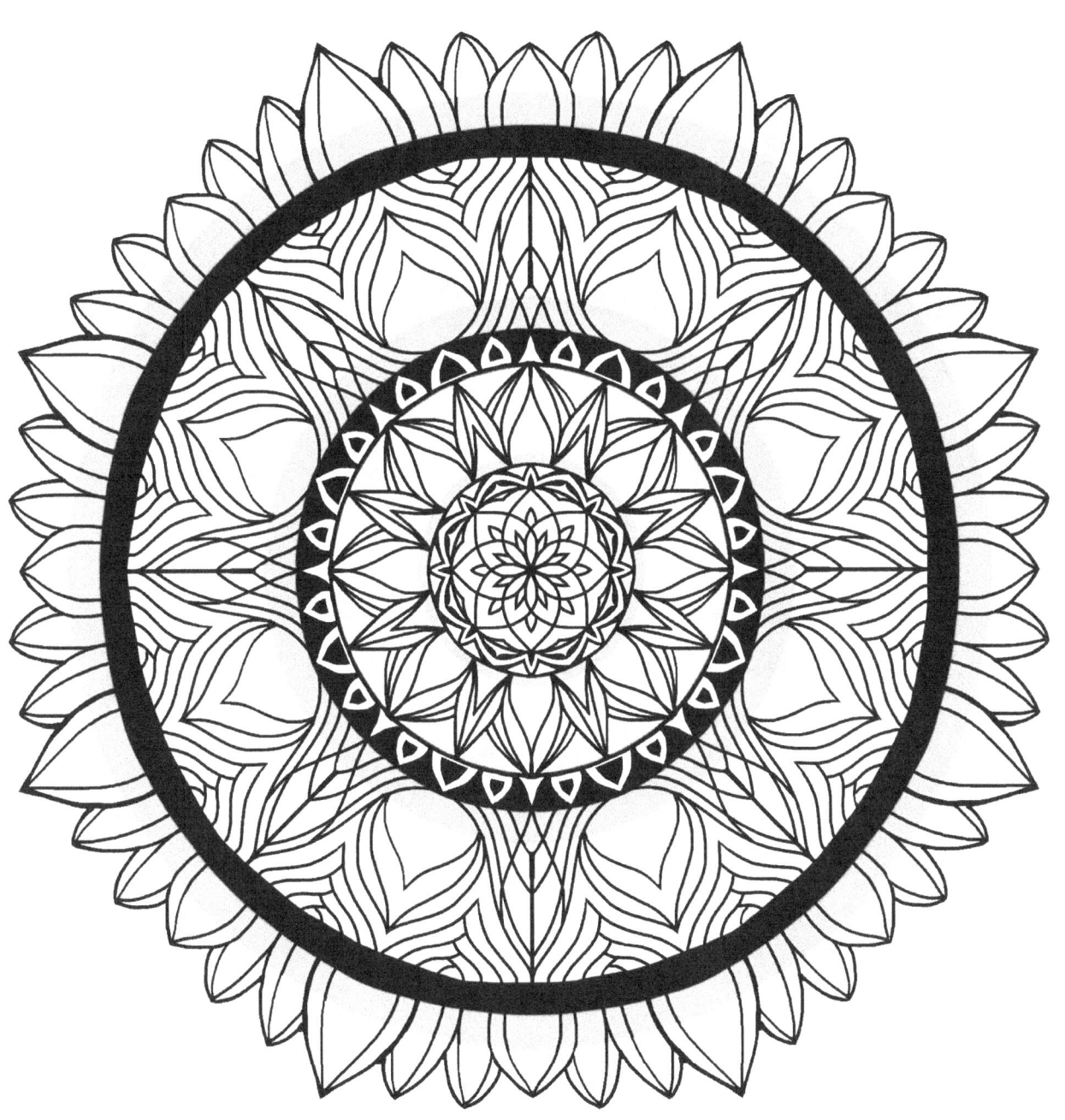

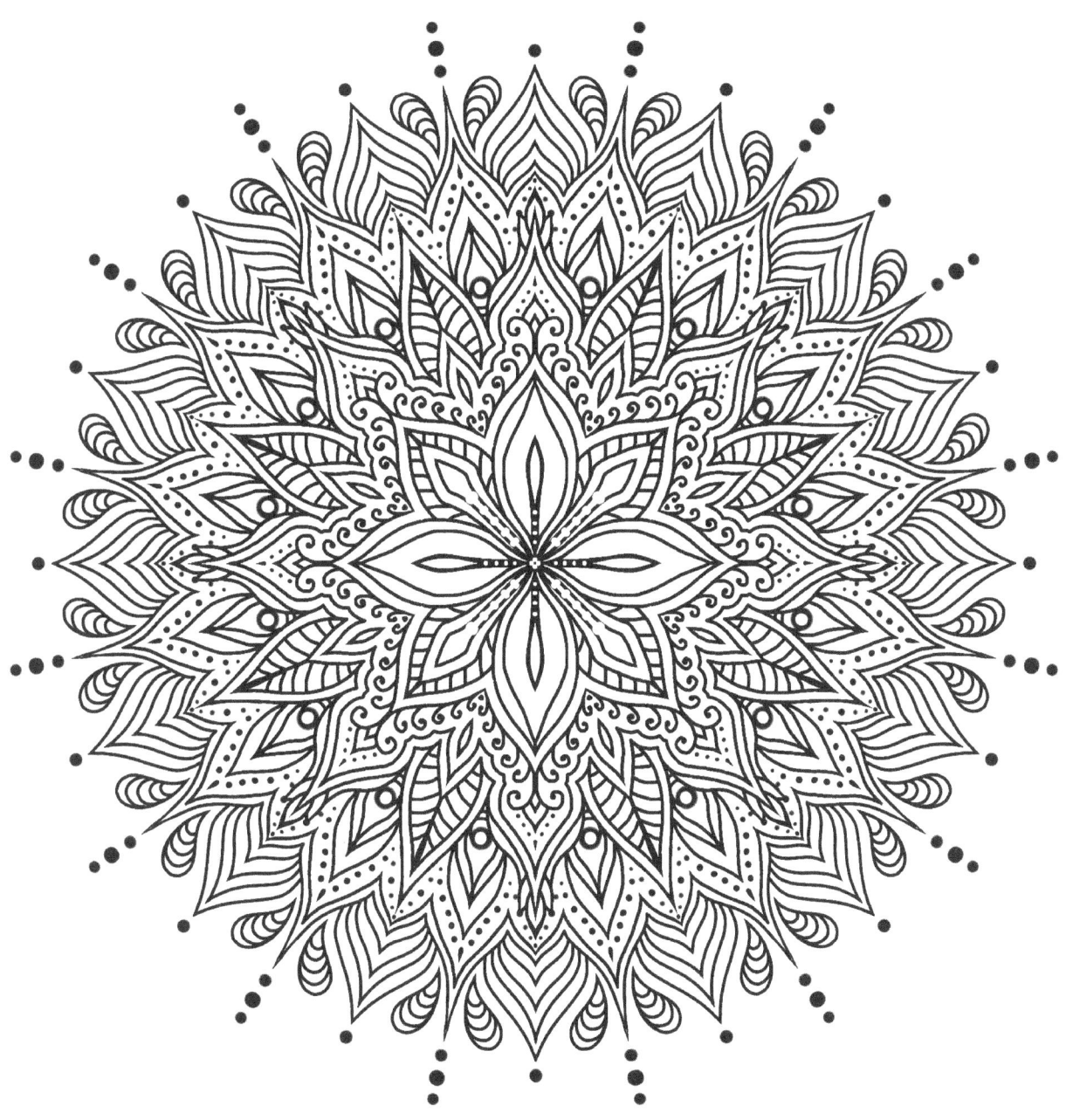

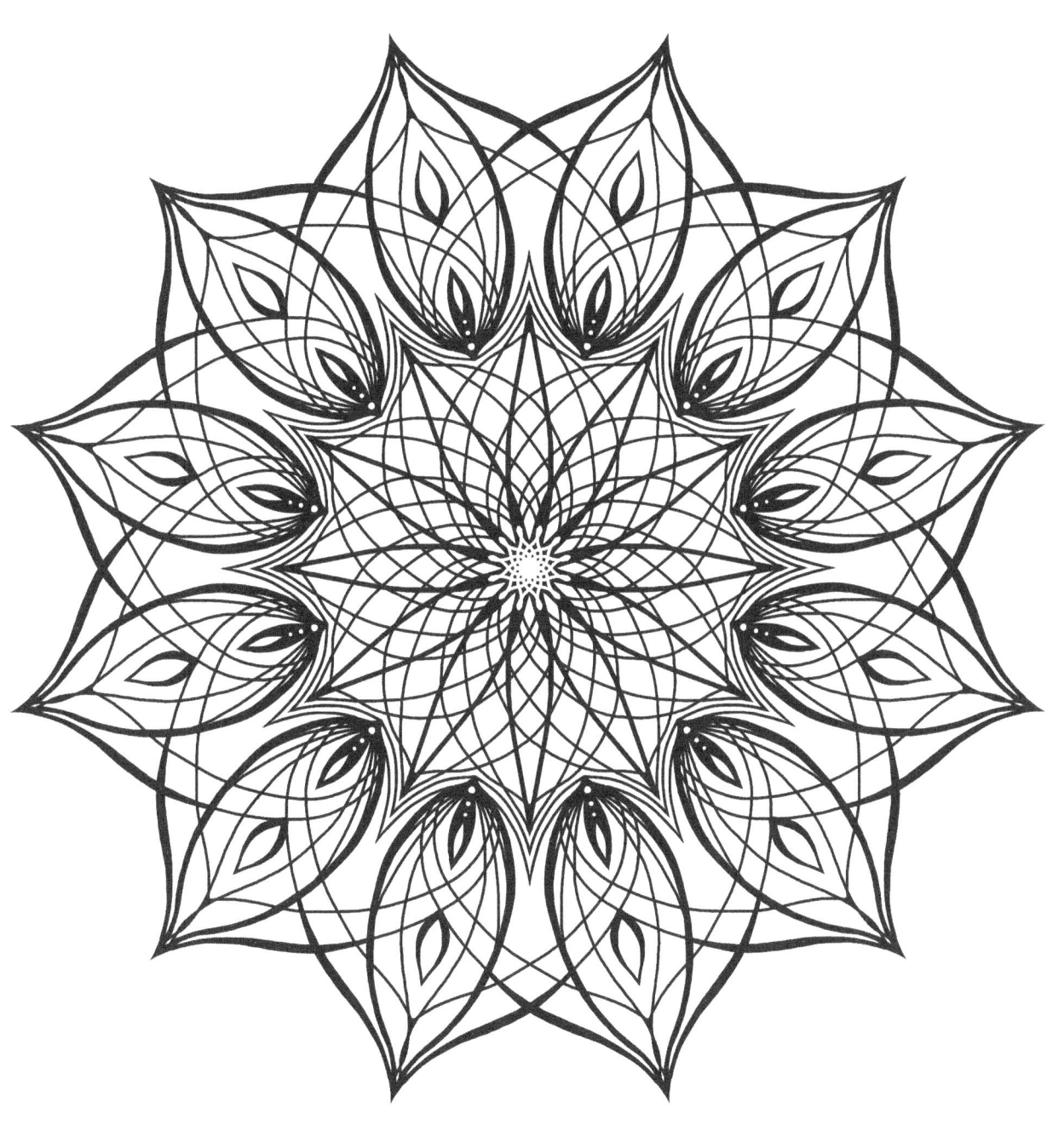

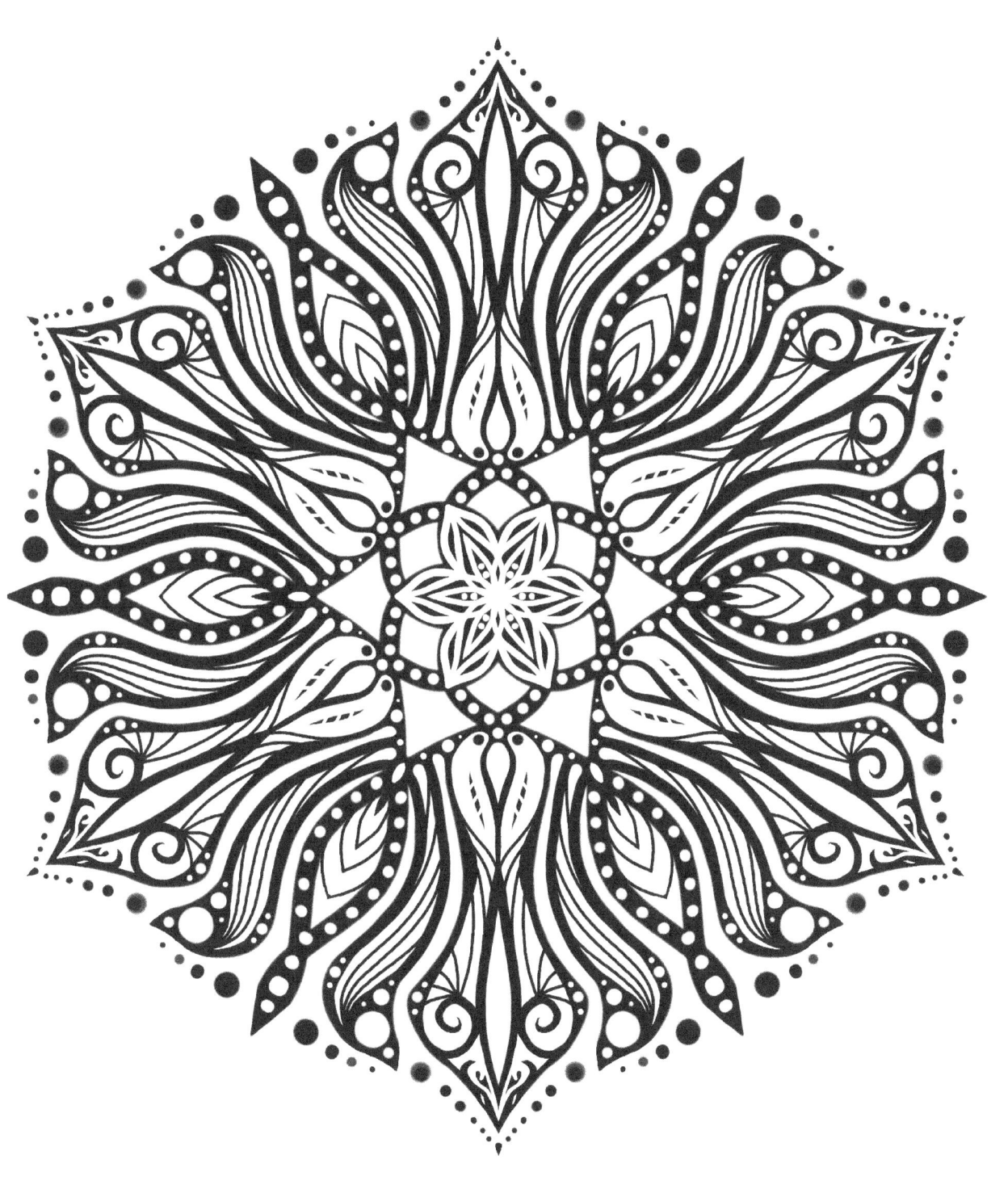

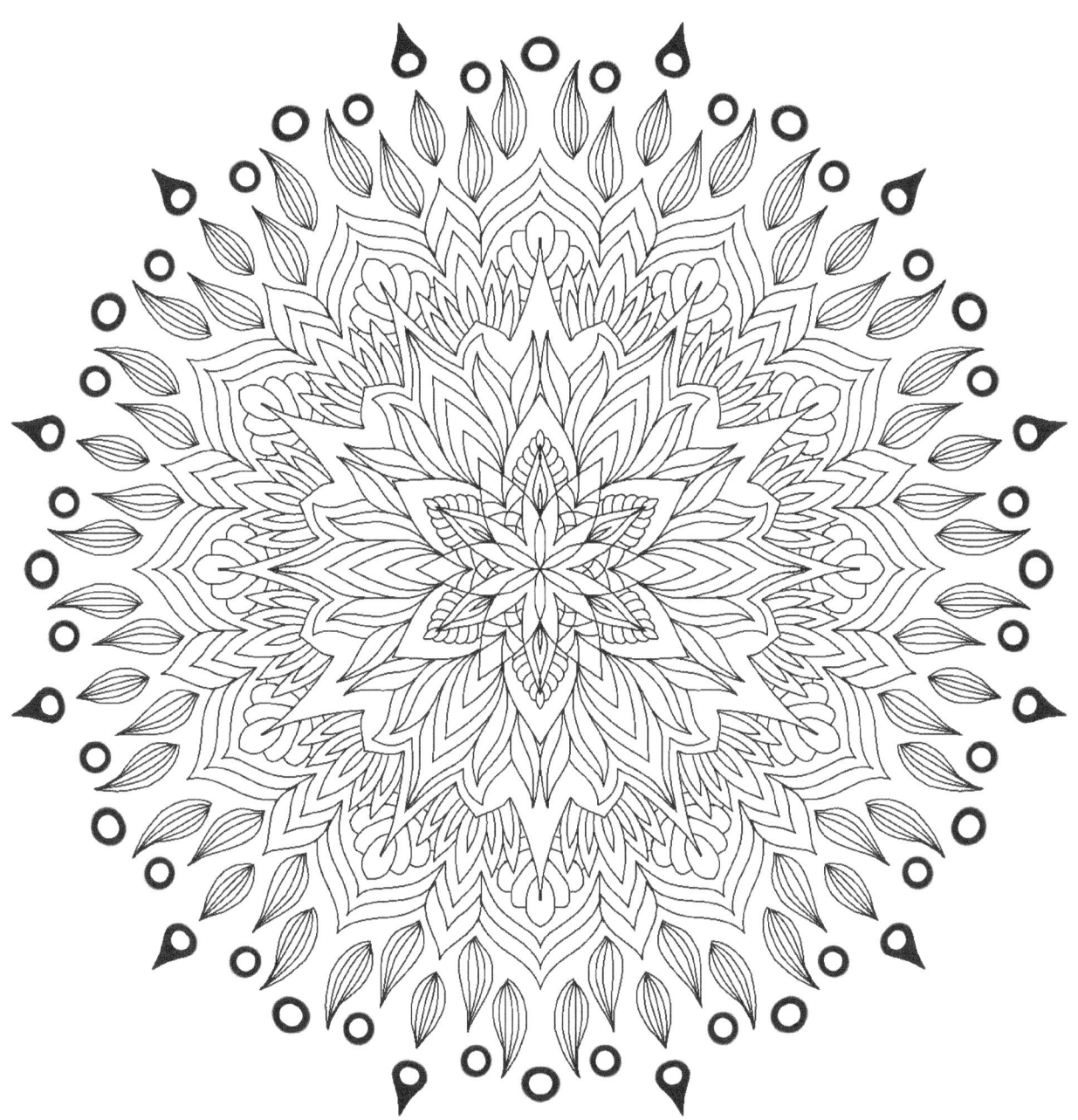

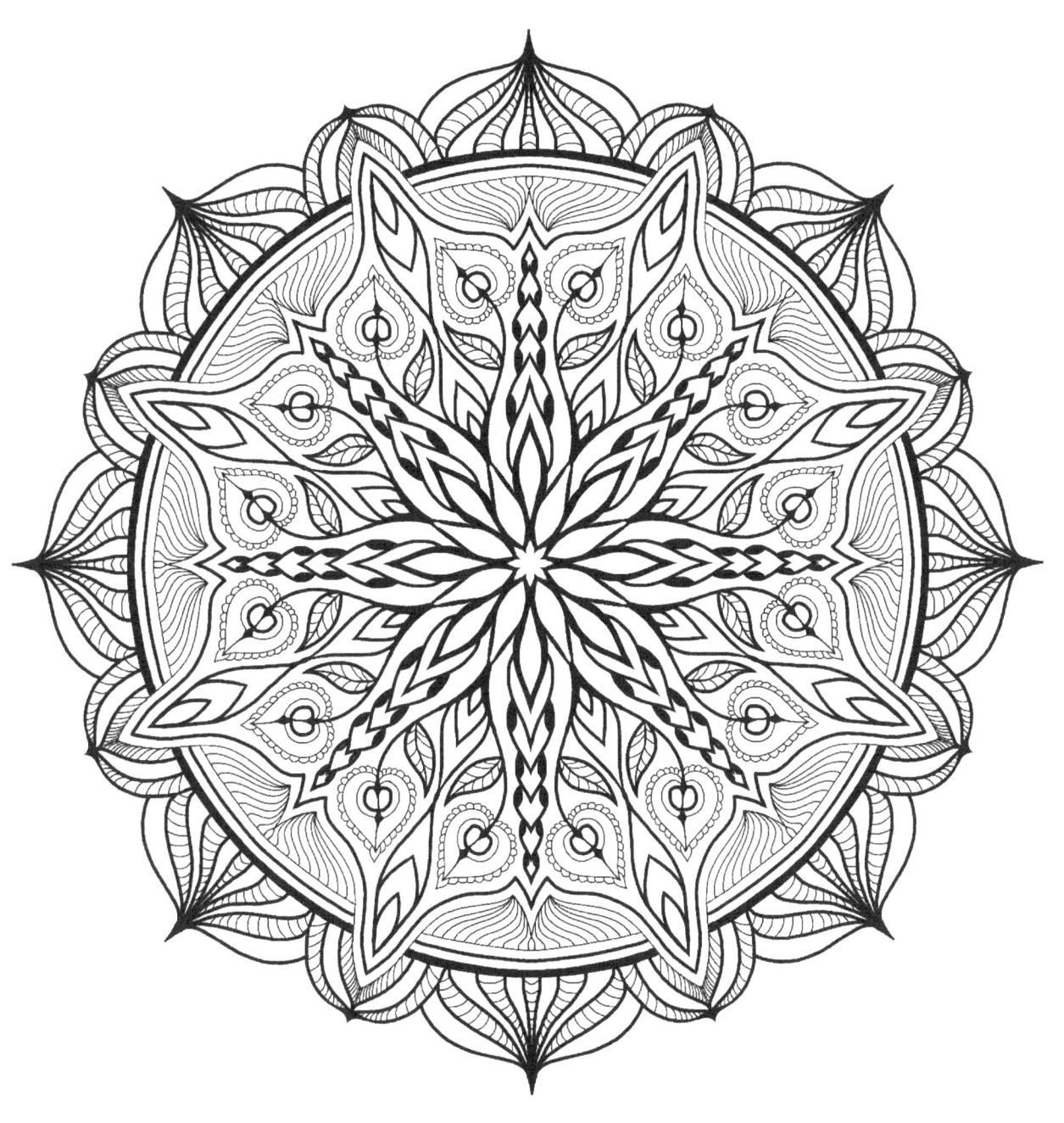

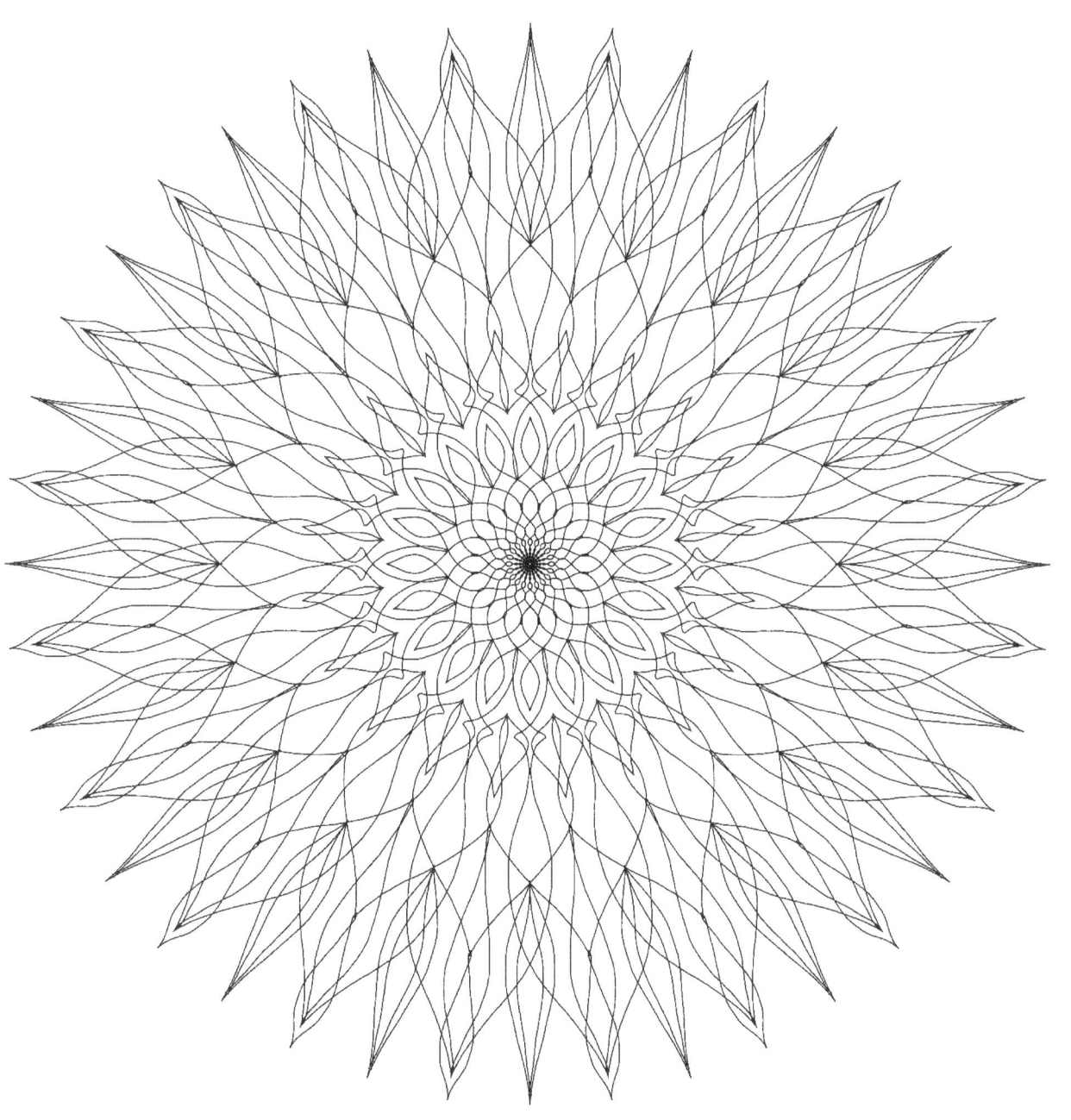

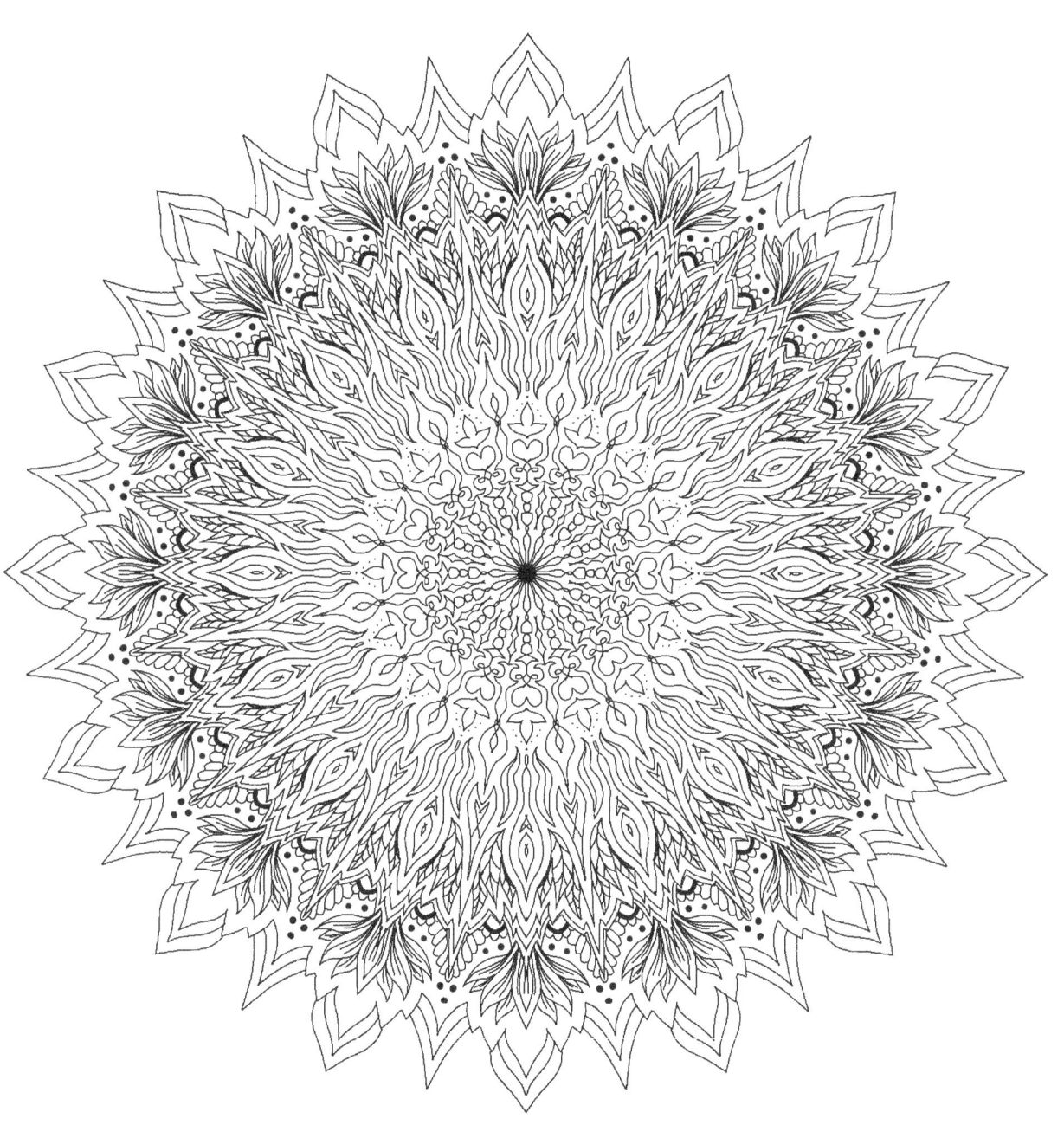

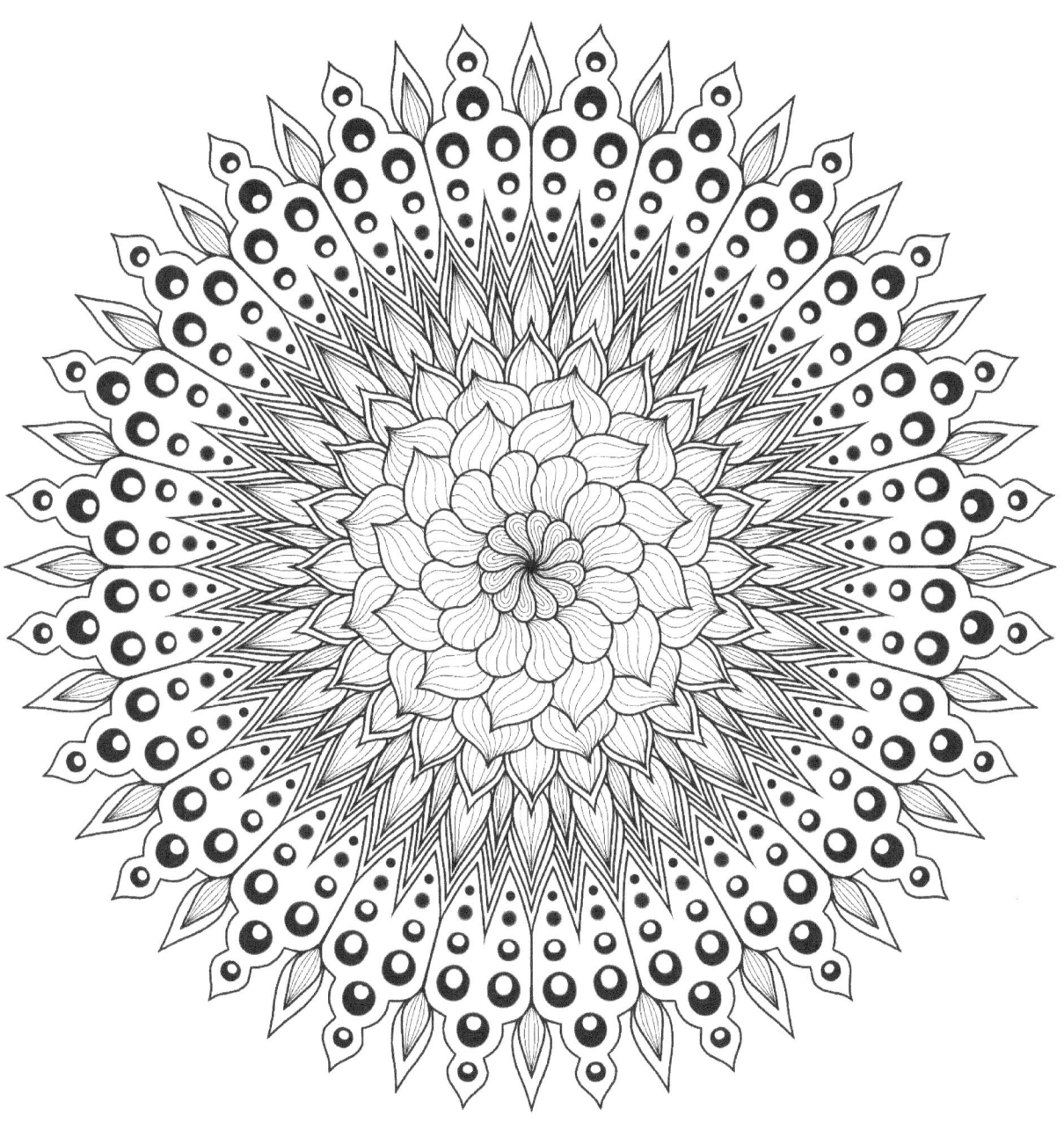

www.ingramcontent.com/pod-product-compliance
Lightning Source LLC
Chambersburg PA
CBHW081223170526
45165CB00009B/2934